STUDIES IN ROMANCE LANGUAGES: 28
John E. Keller, *Editor*

LA DIANA

OF MONTEMAYOR AS SOCIAL & RELIGIOUS TEACHING

Bruno M. Damiani

THE UNIVERSITY PRESS OF KENTUCKY

MIDDLEBURY COLLEGE LIBRARY

Copyright © 1983 by The University Press of Kentucky

Scholarly publisher for the Commonwealth,
serving Bellarmine College, Berea College, Centre
College of Kentucky, Eastern Kentucky University,
The Filson Club, Georgetown College, Kentucky
Historical Society, Kentucky State University,
Morehead State University, Murray State University,
Northern Kentucky University, Transylvania University,
University of Kentucky, University of Louisville,
and Western Kentucky University.

Editorial and Sales Offices: Lexington, Kentucky 40506

Library of Congress Cataloging in Publication Data

Damiani, Bruno Mario.
    La Diana of Montemayor as social and religious
teaching.

    (Studies in Romance languages ; 28)
    Includes index.
    1. Montemayor, Jorge de, 1520?-1561. Diana.
2. Montemayor, Jorge de, 1520?-1561—Political and
social views. 3. Montemayor, Jorge de, 1520?-1561—
Religion and ethics. I. Title. II. Series.
PQ6414.D35 1983 863'.3 83-3608
ISBN 0-8131-1489-6

To my brother, Luigi

Contents

Introduction

Marcelino Menéndez Pelayo, showing both the bias of his times and his own conviction that the pastoral form is decorative rather than meaningful, introduced Montemayor's *Los siete libros de la Diana* (Valencia, 1559) to the twentieth century as an artifice devised by an effete courtly world. Accordingly, he could not conceive of a historical cause for *Diana,* nor even for the appearance of the pastoral novel, which he terms a "puro *dilettantismo* estético."[1] In recent years, however, Rachel Bromberg has taken issue with this view, rightly noting that "no art form arises in a historical void, but is an inevitable embodiment of certain drives, anxieties and satisfactions evoked by the sensibility of the time which produced it, even though this sensibility may be limited to a small group."[2] In fact, in the 1560 edition of *Diana,* dedicated to Lady Barbara Fiesca, Montemayor tells us that the novel originally came to light at the request of certain ladies and gentlemen whom he wished to please.[3] *Diana,* like the genre to which it belongs, was not intended for the masses. It was created for the recreation of a fashionable society amusing itself with amorous accounts of its contemporaries disguised as shepherds and shepherdesses. In this respect *Diana* can well serve to confirm the remark made by one modern critical essayist that "the novel is the private experience of society."[4] Members of the upper classes for whose amusement *Diana* was written took pleasure in unraveling the identity of contemporaries who were portrayed in the disguise of shepherds. Furthermore, as the dramatist Tirso de Molina suggests, intellectuals admired the form and style of *Diana* and other pastoral novels, and women praised the refined sentiments of love contained in them.[5]

Far from being a "pastoral dream" in the sense of a literary creation based on the mythical, *Diana* is a novel with profound sociohistorical dimensions.[6] The immediate and extraordinary success of *Diana* would itself suggest that its entranced readers found things in the book to which they could clearly relate. One thing with which the readers of *Diana* could readily associate themselves was the placidity and tranquillity of life portrayed by the novel and sought so assiduously in the Renaissance as the ideal of happiness.[7] The portrait of a life and nature idealized with an implicit promise of a better life was a source of attraction to readers in "artificial" cities, and such idealization is in itself a part of the reality of *Diana*.[8] The tension, expressed or implied, between town and country values, writes Edward William Tayler, "has always been the source of whatever interest pastoral may possess."[9] The glimpse *Diana* affords of an idyllic nature and of the genuine and profound tenderness shown by Montemayor, notes Ticknor, "introduces a refreshing tone to a society stiff and formal as was that of the Spanish court in the times of Philip II,"[10] in the midst of a culture founded on military virtues and the spirit of knighthood more than any other of modern times.

A principal literary interest of the pastoral novel is its cultivation of the Renaissance ideal of beauty, harmonizing the quietness of an inviting nature with the noble melancholy of human sentiments. The air of melancholy and tears that abounds in *Diana* does not find a ready explanation within the generally exuberant spirit of the Renaissance. The pastoral lament and the suffering and tears of

1. Marcelino Menéndez Pelayo, *Orígenes de la novela* (Santander, 1943), 2: 185.
2. Rachel Bromberg, *Three Pastoral Novels* (Brooklyn, 1969), 12, n. 2.
3. Menéndez Pelayo, *Orígenes de la novela*, 2: 268.
4. Theodore Goodman, *The Techniques of Fiction* (New York, 1955), 27.
5. Cf. Francisco López Estrada, "La *Arcadia* de Lope en la escena de Tirso," *Estudios* 5 (1949): 303-20.
6. Cf. Francisco López Estrada, "La epístola de Jorge de Montemayor a Diego Ramírez Pagán," *Estudios dedicados a Menéndez Pidal* 6 (1956): 388.
7. Cf. Francesco de Sanctis, *Storia della letteratura Italiana* (Salani, n.d.) 1: 468.
8. J.E. Varey, "La campagne dans le théatre espagnol au XVIIe siècle," in *Dramaturgie et société*, ed. Jean Jacquot (Paris, 1968), 75.
9. Edward William Tayler, *Nature and Art in Renaissance Literature* (New York, 1967), 69.
10. George Ticknor, *History of Spanish Literature* (Boston, 1849), 3: 54.

those disguised shepherds have all been linked to what Américo Castro has called the "edad conflictiva" of the sixteenth century, the age of inner conflict felt by the New Christians, a conflict created by the felt inferiority of the Jews and Arabs who had embraced the new faith.[11] The idealistic representation of man and nature inherent in pastoral literature provided a more verifiable link with sociohistorical circumstances, as it clashed with the orthodox spirit of the time, becoming often the object of intense criticism by moralists, who saw its portrayal of life as deleterious to man's quest for God. The concomitant result was often the writing and rewriting of pastoral novels in the form of religious allegories, as was done by Brother Bartolomé Ponce, the Cistercian monk from Aragon, when he wrote a contrafactum of Montemayor's novel, entitling it *Clara Diana a lo divino*.

By the first half of the sixteenth century the fictional shepherd attained an expanded artistic function in relation to himself (i.e., greater description of his office and the tools of his work), to his surroundings (greater association between the shepherd and the bucolic setting), and to the characters around him (more dialogue).[12] The shepherd also achieved an amplified role in spiritual terms by becoming a moralizer. This is seen, for example, in the humanistic treatise called *El Deseoso* (1515), in which several shepherds ably expound a variety of moral and doctrinal questions to the astonishment of the major character, Deseoso, an inquisitive and wandering monk.[13] Shepherds are seen as wise in matters of morality and ethics. One of the characters in Jerónimo de Contreras's *Selva de Aventuras* reflects upon a dramatic representation of shepherds'

11. Américo Castro, *De la edad conflictiva* (Madrid, 1961), 17–21. See also Marcel Bataillon, "¿Melancolía renacentista o melancolía judía?" in *Varia lección de clásicos españoles* (Madrid, 1964), 39–53.

12. The role of the shepherd in Renaissance literature is examined at length by Francisco López Estrada in his authoritative volume *Los libros de pastores en la literatura española: La órbita previa* (Madrid, 1974).

13. On this outstanding treatise of spirituality, cf. Francisco López Estrada, "Érasme et les origines de l'idéal pastoral en Espagne: le Traité *El Deseoso*," in *Actas del XII Stage International d'Etudes Humanistes*, University of Orleans-Tours (Paris, 1972), 1: 503–14; see also idem, *Notas sobre la espiritualidad española de los Siglos de Oro: Estudio del "Tratado llamado el Deseoso,"* Universidad de Sevilla, 1972.

amorous contentions and reports that one Luzmán was left totally fulfilled after having seen this play. He saw how beneath those things which seemed frivolous and entertaining there lay good advice, and so, we are told, he praised the story, especially its moral message.[14]

Morality and didacticism are deeply-rooted aspects of Montemayor's entire literary production, from his *Diálogo spiritual* and *Glosa de diez coplas de Jorge Manrique,* through his allegorical dramatic trilogy and the devotional poetry of the *Cancionero,* to the *Carta de los trabajos de los reyes* and his pastoral novel, *Diana.* It is precisely this sustained spirituality, betrayed from his earliest works, that led Rodrigo de Mendoza to say of Montemayor, "De oy más, serás llamado, en nuestra España, el gran poeta christiano."[15] The consistent and well defined pattern demonstrated in various of Montemayor's works for the theological exposition of the doctrines of faith, hope, and charity, the mysteries of incarnation and the promise of redemption, and praise of the Blessed Virgin, reveals the author's adherence to the principle that literature can and should be a vehicle for moral didacticism.

The condition of *otiosus,* proper to the shepherd after his characterization in Virgil's *Bucolics* took on a spiritual meaning early in the Christian era, acquired a connotation that came to be often associated with the contemplative state.[16] Because of this, writers of the Middle Ages and the Renaissance found pastoral literature a particularly viable vehicle for evangelization. This may be seen in the fourth-century pastoral poem *De Mortibus Boum* by St. Severus and in the two eclogues of the French writer and bishop Modoin de Autun, written between the years 800 and 814. Significantly, Modoin's eclogues were also the first works in which an author himself proclaimed the existence of a hidden meaning in pastoral

14. Jerónimo de Contreras, *Selva de aventuras* (Barcelona, 1565), *Biblioteca de Autores Españoles* 3: 474.

15. Sonnet by Rodrigo de Mendoza, in Jorge de Montemayor, *Segundo cancionero spiritual* (Antwerp, 1558), 1, cited by Mario Martins, "Uma obra inédita de Jorge de Montemōr," *Brotería* 43 (1946): 400.

16. Francisco López Estrada, "Los temas de la pastoril antigua," *Anales de la Universidad Hispalense* 28 (1967): 41.

literature.[17] That hidden meaning was underscored by Theodolus, a little-known author of the tenth century who, combining Greek myth with Biblical stories, produced a spiritual eclogue in which shepherds appear as allegorical shepherds defending Christian beliefs against the tide of superstitions.[18] In Petrarch's words, "allegory is not only essential in poetry: allegory is the very substance of poetry."[19] In accordance with this principle, Petrarch wrote his twelve eclogues, declaring that they could only be understood with a key. Petrarch's detailed declaration made to his brother Gerardo, a Carthusian monk,[20] is, in the words of Francisco López Estrada, "extraordinariamente ejemplar"[21] for it underscores the potential for spiritual allegory inherent in much of pastoral literature.

The transcendental nature of the pastoral is emphasized by Walter W. Greg as he explains the importation of foreign matters into the spontaneous lyric beauty of the pastoral setting:

The pastoral, whatever its form, always needed and assumed some external circumstances to give point to its actual content. The interest seldom arises directly from the narrative itself. In Theocritus and Sannazzaro this objective point is supplied by the delight of escape from the over-civilization of the city; in Petrarch and Mantuan, by their allegorical intention; in Sacchetti and Lorenzo, by the contrast of town and city, with all its delicate humour; in Boccaccio and Poliziano, by the opening it gave for golden dreams of exquisite beauty or sensual delight; in Tasso, by the desire of that freedom in love and life which sentimental philosophers have always asso-

17. Frank Russell Hamblin, *The Development of Allegory in the Classical Pastoral* (Menasha, Wis., 1928), 64–65, cited by López Estrada, *Los libros de pastores*, 41.

18. Ernst R. Curtius, *European Literature and the Latin Middle Ages* (New York, 1953), 49f, 51 and n., 220, 221 and n., 446.

19. *Epistolae de Rebus Familiaribus*, ed. G. Fracassetti (Florence, 1859), 2: 83.

20. Francesco Petrarca, *Le familiari*, 11.10.4, ed. V. Rossi (Florence, 1934), 301-10. See Enrico Carrara, *La poesia pastorale* (Milan, n.d.), 87-111, in which the *Bucolicum carmen* is studied. Cf. López Estrada, "Los temas de la pastoril," 131-82.

21. López Estrada, "Los temas de la pastoril," 48.

ciated with a return to nature. In all these cases the content *per se* may be said to be a matter of indifference; it only receives meaning in relation to some ulterior intention of the author.[22]

That intention is clothed in symbolism which does not, however, conceal the artist's perception of life, for, as Wallace Fowlie reminds us, "symbolism in art does not hide the artist's experience; rather it reveals it, considering it in its relationship with the experience of humanity."[23]

22. Walter W. Greg, *Pastoral Poetry and Pastoral Drama* (London, 1906), 27.

23. Wallace Fowlie, *The Clown's Grail: A Study of Love in Its Literary Expression* (London, 1948), 8.

Chapter One

Social and Historical Realities

Spain, the mother of the modern novel, fostered pastoral literature to an unparalleled degree throughout the sixteenth and seventeenth centuries. The unique success of books about shepherds in Spain can be attributed to the readers' appreciation of the esthetic and moral values disclosed in that literature, but also—and fundamentally so—to the esteem in which was held the work of shepherds, that "noble oficio pastoril"[1] discussed with such enthusiasm by Gabriel Alonso de Herrera in his volume on *Agricultura general* (1513). Praise of shepherds and the rural world had also come from Aristotle, who proclaimed that a farming and pastoral society was the only one able to sustain a system of democracy without the danger of corruption (*Politics,* 6.2).

The novel's aim, notes Georg Lukács, is "to represent a particular social reality at a particular time, with all the colour and specific atmosphere of the time."[2] In *Diana* the interaction of fiction and history is far greater than has been noted thus far. The characters either are shepherds or disguise themselves as shepherds, not of an imaginary Arcadian land, but rather of Spain (or Portugal) itself. In contrast to Virgil, "who was said to have deliberately placed in the mouths of his herdsmen geographical statements that are false or confusing"[3] (e.g., Eclogue 2.24), Montemayor has his shepherds present a catalogue of accurate and readily identifiable locations. Most of the action of the novel takes place in the fields of León by the banks of the river Esla (7)[4] where there begins a glade, ideal as a cattle path, that extends to the river Duero and beyond to the Tajo river not far from the Portuguese border.[5] In this respect Montemayor's work reflects what Américo Castro has called "integralismo hispánico,"[6] the desire of the Spaniard to live on his own soil, to be identified with it.

Following the example of migratory movement set by Torquemada's pastoral dialogue of 1552, in which shepherds come down from the mountains with their flocks to the plains, Sireno "baxaba de las montañas de León . . . a los verdes y deleitosos prados" (9)[7] of the dale below. From there, he and the other shepherds and shepherdesses whom he meets move from one dale to another until they reach Felicia's palace. When they eventually take leave of the palace they all go back to caring for their flocks in the lush glens.

As Theocritus had done before him, Montemayor uses the pastoral form to praise his homeland. In Book VII of *Diana*, through Felismena, he describes the Portuguese countryside near Coimbra, "una de las más insignes y principales [ciudades] de aquel reyno y aún de toda la Europa," we are told, a city bathed by the "cristalinas aguas [del] Mondego." Standing in the foreground is the historical castle of "Monte moro vello" (the birthplace of Montemayor), where force of genius, valor, and courage have remained, in the words of the author, as "tropheos de las hazañas que los habitadores dél . . . avían hecho" (287). The valiant deeds to which Montemayor refers here are the legendary exploits of Abbot Don Juan of Montemayor, whose feats have been discussed best by Menéndez Pidal.[8] In her contemplation of Coimbra and the surrounding countryside, Felismena departs from what has been, in this work and in previous pastoral novels, the description of a uniform and monotonous

1. Werner Krauss, "Localización y desplazamiento en la novela pastoril española," in *Actas del Segundo Congreso Internacional de Hispanistas*, ed. Jaime Sánchez Romeralo and Norbert Poulussen (Nijmegen, 1967), 365.

2. Georg Lukács, *The Historical Novel* (Baltimore, 1969), 177.

3. Thomas G. Rosenmeyer, *The Green Cabinet: Theocritus and the European Pastoral Lyric* (Berkeley, 1969), 115.

4. For the geographical background of the historical *Diana*, see Albano Garcia Abad, "Sobre la patria de la *Diana*," *Revista de literatura* 27 (1965): 67–77. Unless otherwise noted, all textual references to *Diana* are based on the edition prepared by Francisco López Estrada (Madrid, 1946).

5. Krauss, "Localización," 367.

6. Américo Castro, *La realidad histórica de España*, 2nd ed. (Mexico, 1962), I, 92.

7. Cited by Krauss, "Localización," 367.

8. See Ramón Menéndez Pidal, "La leyenda del abad don Juan de Montemayor," in Menéndez Pidal's *Historia y epopeya* (Madrid, 1934), 98–233, a condensed version of which appears in his *Poesia árabe y poesia europea* (Madrid, 1941), 159–209.

setting to inject a measure of proportion and an indication of distance: a plain "twelve miles" long, fields "three miles" wide (281), walking "six miles" by the banks of the river (282). The characters of the novel are from real places. Selvagia was born in Portugal in the region flanked by two rivers, one of which is the Duero (40). The business of Selvagia's father takes him to the region of Estremadura, given the learned name of "Estremo" in the text (51). Alanio is from Galia, a village three miles from Selvagia's town (46). The nymphs cross the "puertos Galizianos" (93) on their way back to Felicia's palace. Felismena was born in Spain in a city called Soldina in Vandalia (95-96), probable toponyms for Seville and Andalusia, respectively.[9] Following their mother's death, Felismena and her brother, children of nobility, are brought up in a convent (99).

Diana offers at least one exception to the pastoral norm that deprives herdsmen of the advantages of education and status, by portraying Arsileo, son of a shepherd, as a student going off to the University of Salamanca to become an accomplished poet and musician. The musical talent of Arsileo is revealed by the following comment: "y [Belisa] estando atenta, vió cómo el pastor començó a tocar el rabel tan divinamente, que parecía cosa del cielo; y aviendo tañido un poco con una voz más angélica que de hombre humano, dió principio a esta canción" (231). The eye-catching reference to Arsileo's voice as "más angélica que de hombre humano" could itself betray an interesting sociological reality by its possible allusion to the singing of castrati, popular in the sixteenth century, with voices often described as "rare" and "delicate."[10] In this regard, it is worth noting the way a critic of the eighteenth century writes about a leading castrato of his time, Pauluccio, of Rome: "This eunuch, who was then about nineteen years of age, was indeed the wonder of the world. For besides that his voice was higher than anyone else's, it had all the warblings of a nightingale, but with only this difference, that it was much finer; and did not a man know the

---

9. Narciso Alonso Cortés, "Sobre Montemayor y la *Diana*," *Artículos histórico-literarios* (Valladolid, 1935), 134–38.

10. I owe this observation to the distinguished musicologist Richard Sherr, of Smith College, whose letter to me, dated May 1, 1981, includes also considerable bibliographical information on sixteenth-century music.

contrary, he would believe it impossible such a tone could proceed from the throat of anything that was human."[11]

As a final tribute to the art of the castrati may be cited the opinion of the musical historian Enrico Panzacchi (1840-1904), who, late in the nineteenth century, heard with ecstasy one of the surviving castrati in the papal chapel: "What singing! Imagine a voice that combines the sweetness of the flute, and the animated suavity of the human larynx—a voice which leaps and leaps, lightly and spontaneously, like a lark that flies through the air and is intoxicated with its own flight; . . . in a word, a voice that gives the immediate idea of sentiment transmuted into sound, and of the ascension of a soul into the infinite on the wings of that sentiment."[12] The presence in *Diana* of a possible allusion to the "angelic" music of castrati may add an important historical and artistic dimension to the novel, heretofore unnoticed, making *Diana* one of the first literary works to allude to that type of voice, which emerged only in the middle of the sixteenth century. Worth noting in terms of Montemayor's ethnic background and his association with the Spanish and Portuguese courts is the fact that the use of castrati in Portugal is recorded during the reign of Don Sebastian (1557-78). In the sixteenth century Portugal's eunuchs were apparently imported from Italy, which in turn got most, if indeed not all, its castrati from Spain.[13] The fame of the castrati, often referred to as "songbirds," reached its highest point in the eighteenth century, when castrati "were discussed, compared, and criticized in fashionable drawing-rooms . . . from Russia to Portugal and from Ireland to the borders of the Ottoman Empire."[14] In essence, then, *Diana* could serve again to illustrate the view that pastoral literature "plays a distinct and a distinctive part in the history of human thoughts and the history of artistic expression."[15]

11. Henry Pleasants, *The Great Singers from the Dawn of Opera to Our Own Time* (New York, 1966), 42.

12. Angus Heriot, *The Castrati in Opera* (New York, 1974), 36–37.

13. See Richard Sherr, "Guglielmo Gonzaga and the Castrati," *Renaissance Quarterly* 30 (1980): 33–56. Cf. Angus Heriot, *Castrati in Opera,* 11, 15.

14. Heriot, *Castrati in Opera,* 13.

15. Walter G. Greg, "Pastoral: A Literary Inquiry," in *Pastoral and Romance,* ed. Eleanor Terry Lincoln (Englewood Cliffs, N. J., 1969), 8.

The setting of the pastoral novel, which was without place and time for most of the pastoral tradition from classical antiquity to the early sixteenth century, becomes to a significant degree in *Diana* an abstract, a microcosm of life. As such, *Diana* serves well to illustrate what Ramón Menéndez Pidal has referred to as the Spaniards' inclination toward art for life rather than art for art's sake; in Spanish writings, he notes, literature and life interweave much more closely than they do in the literary works of other countries, since Spanish man is basically "idealista y poético."[16] Like specific references to place names and spatial perspective, the chronological approach illustrates the novel's connection with a finite historical system. Belisa's relationship with Arsenio lasts "más de quatro años" (137). Following the concocted deaths of Arsileo and Arsenio, Belisa passes exactly six months in solitude before being found by the shepherds and nymphs on their way to Felicia's palace (159). Danteo is told by his father that he must marry within three days (284). Fabio's reference to St. Martin's wine alludes to the first vintage of the year, which was opened on St. Martin's day, November 11.[17]

Montemayor endowed time "with new meanings that greatly expand the world of the novel and enhance its ability to reflect 'human time' with artistic fidelity":[18] "E de ay a ocho días" (47), "passado un mes" (114), "mas siendo ya passada media noche" (43), "y porque ya eran más de tres horas de la noche" (161), "la mañana se vino" (46), "y siendo ya hora de levantarme" (110). In addition, the rhythm of life is maintained by repeated references to sunrise and sunset, and to the heat of the afternoon, when shepherds and shepherdesses unfailingly take a respite from their pastoral chores under the shade of the tranquillity-inducing alder trees in order to ameliorate the grief brought on by unrequited love. *Diana*'s attention to particulars of space, time, and shepherds' activities fulfills the requirements of the novel, set forth by Georg Lukács, as an art form that "must penetrate into the small details of everyday life,

16. Ramón Menéndez Pidal, *Los españoles en la literatura* (Madrid, 1971), 48.
17. RoseAnna M. Mueller, "Montemayor's *Diana*: A Translation and Introduction" (Ph.D. diss., New York University, 1977), 162, n. 14.
18. Joseph R. Jones, "'Human Time' in *La Diana*," *Romance Notes* 10 (1968): 146.

into the concrete time of the action, it must bring out what is specific to this time through the complex interaction of all these details."[19]

However fictitious this interaction may seem in *Diana,* it is interwoven with a human experience well known to its readers.[20] The lexicon of the shepherd that includes "rebaño" (282), "çurrón" (9), and "cayado" (30) was very much a part of the social and economic order of the time. As Werner Krauss points out, the pastoral profession in fifteenth- and sixteenth-century Spain enjoyed the special favor of governments, in contrast to agriculture, which was completely abandoned. Monetary considerations pressed the rulers into concentrating the national economy on the production of wool.[21] The importance of shepherds' work was manifested, furthermore, by the establishment of a shepherds' union, called the Mesta, endowed with very special privileges that included judicial powers and exemption from military service for shepherds. Pacifism, a profoundly Renaissance and Erasmian concern, was typified by the life of shepherds, and eulogies written in defense of shepherds' organizations often relied on bucolic writings to sustain their thesis.[22] At one point the orthodox Caja de Leruela, a leader of the shepherds' union, even invoked Pan, god-protector of shepherds, to help its members prosper.[23]

Montemayor's novel is not without references to the prosperity of the pastoral community. Andronio and Delia, Felismena's parents, are "en linaje y bienes de fortuna, los más principales de aquella provincia [de Soldina, i.e. Sevilla]" (97). Selvagia comes from Portugal, from a fertile land with many houses, forests, many hard-working inhabitants, and a close-knit community (40). Belisa seems to derive from an even more prosperous area than does Selvagia. Her village is in a forest near two rivers, and the houses are

19. Georg Lukács, *Historical Novel,* 177.
20. López Estrada, *Los libros de pastores,* 282.
21. Krauss, "Localización," 366. See also Julius Klein, *The Mesta: A Study in Spanish Economic History 1273-1836,* Cambridge, Mass., 1920.
22. Krauss, "Localización," 363–69.
23. Caja de Leruela, *Restauración de la abundancia de España* (1631), cited in ibid., 365.

set so thick together "que desde una casa, la otra no se parece" (136). The houses are surrounded with fragrant gardens, "de olorosas flores, de más de la abundancia de la ortaliza que allí la naturaleza produze, ayudada de la industria de los moradores" (136). The people there are free and of old lineage. Belisa lives in a house large enough to have "una açotea alta" (150), surely no peasant's hovel. Her admirer, Arsenio, is "un pastor de los principales en hazienda y linage que en toda esta provincia se hallava" (136). He is well enough off to send his son, Arsileo, to the university to acquire graces and an education at a time when small farmers and shepherd communities needed the help of all members of the family to remain solvent. Arsenio tries to win the love of Belisa by flooding her with presents, "joyas y otras muchas cosas" (146).

Prosperity is also apparent in the description of Delio as an uncouth man who, although "rico de los bienes de fortuna, no lo es de los de naturaleza" (30), such as talent for singing, playing, and dancing, a fact, which makes him an outcast to both pastoral and courtly societies.[24] The only motivation the shepherds can find for Diana's change from sorrow at Sireno's departure to willingness to marry Delio is the latter's wealth.[25] In contrast to the opinion expressed by Jacqueline Savoye de Ferreras that the characters of *Diana* are oblivious to money,[26] at least one character, Selvagia's father, is apparently quite concerned with it as he is reported carrying out the business of setting the boundaries of certain pastures with the shepherd Filenio (51). In this respect Selvagia's father gives credence to the arguments of Thrasymachus and Callicles, Socrates' partners, that a shepherd must not only have the welfare of his flock at heart but must, like a ruler, look after his own interests in order to be successful.[27] For this, it is not altogether correct to share the view of Amadeu Solé-Leris that *Diana*'s characters are so preoccupied as lovers that they are "undistracted by social, economic,

24. For a superb insight into social values implicit in the pastoral genre, see William Empson, *English Pastoral Poetry* (New York, 1938).
25. Cf. Michele Ricciardelli, *Gil Polo, Montemayor e Sannazaro* (Montevideo, 1966), 10.
26. Jacqueline Savoye de Ferreras, "El mito del pastor," *Cuadernos Hispanoamericanos* 308 (1976): 40.
27. Rosenmeyer, *Green Cabinet,* 99.

or other considerations."[28] A reference to ownership is made again when Arsenio, learning of Belisa's disappearance, retires to a piece of secluded property he owns (257).

Prosperity depends on work, and in this reinforces the fact that amidst the overwhelming preoccupation with love which characterizes all of *Diana*'s shepherds and shepherdesses, there is also present a concern for the shepherds' real task of caring for flocks.[29] References to the characters' role as working shepherds abound in *Diana.* Following a lengthy lament against his loved one at the beginning of the first book, Sireno suddenly realizes that he has neglected all his "hato y rebaño" (18). Described with a "sayal tan áspero como su ventura, un cayado en la mano, un çurrón del braço yzquierdo colgando" (10), Sireno later "recoge su ganado" and takes it to pasture on the mountains of León (74). Meanwhile, Diana is seen bringing her flock to the river (20), and at sunset she takes her flock back to her village (26).

At the high point of their relationship Sireno and Diana forget their sheep and lambs and think instead of each other "hablando ella comigo y yo mirándola" (33), thus supplying the novel with a profoundly human dimension. Selvagia takes to pasture a few goats that were tied up in a pen near her house just after Alanio sees her bringing her sheep to the fold (52). Besides the sheep and goats mentioned, some of the rustics keep cattle along with their other animals—dogs (269) and horses (105, 110, 294, 299)—pointing up the fact that in pastoral literature, unlike the fable or the Gothic tale, animals are true animals.[30] The word bucolic, so often applied to the setting of *Diana,* is itself highly suggestive. It derives from the Greek *boukolos,* a keeper of cattle as opposed to a shepherd or goatherd, and represents an enhancement of the social status of the figures of pastoral poetry.

Pastoral life is vividly portrayed in Book II of *Diana,* where shepherds are seen leading their "mansas ovejuelas" to "espessos

28. Amadeu Solé-Leris, *The Spanish Pastoral Novel* (Boston, 1980), 35–36.

29. The examples of pastoral life that follow have also been cited by José Siles Artés, who provides a brief but useful look into the real pastoral life of shepherds in *Diana* in *El arte de la novela pastoril* (Valencia, 1972), 103–5.

30. Rosenmeyer, *Green Cabinet,* 133.

bosques" near the "cristalinas aguas" of the Esla river (63). Sylvano is with his flock among the "myrthos que cerca de la fuente avía" (66). The pastoral sketch is enriched with Belisa's description of herself and her companions sitting around a spring while their cows graze in the shade of tall trees and lick their young heifers (150). At other times "las pastoras andavan ocupadas con sus vacas, atándoles sus mansos bezerillos a los pies, y dexándose ellas engañar de la industria humana" (155) to the end, apparently, that the cows would believe their offspring to be hungry and about to feed and would more freely release their milk to the ministrations of the young ladies.

Following the long parenthesis of events in Felicia's palace (Book IV), the rustics are once again depicted in their customary activity as shepherds. Thus in Book V Sylvano and Selvagia "caminavan hazia el deleitoso prado donde sus ganados andavan paciendo" (238). Even Diana is seen searching for a lamb that has strayed from her flock (265), adding a realistic detail to the standard action of shepherds passively looking after their flocks. Then, in the novel's final book, as Felismena enters into Portugal, she meets two shepherdesses in full pastoral activity :"levantándose la una con grande priessa a echar una manada de ovejas de un linar a donde se avían entrado, y la otra, llegado a bever a un rebaño de cabras al claro río, se bolvieron a la sombra del umbroso fresno" (282). Significantly, the physical appearance of these shepherdesses is minutely described in "realistic" terms. They do not have the idealized images of men and women created by courtly poets but are simply rustic figures of only average beauty, "hermosura [de] razonable medianía," "rostro moreno" with "ojos negros" and "cabellos no muy ruvios" (282). Consistent with their national origin, these shepherdesses speak Portuguese and offer a concrete sketch of life in the western part of the Iberian peninsula.

Parenthetically, it is worth noting that in Portugal rich vegetation replaces the conventional green grass of the previous setting. The Portuguese shepherd Danteo says to Duarda, "Eu yrie en tanto a repastar teu gado, e terei conta con que as ovellas não entren nas searas que a longo desta ribeira estão" (291). In the last three books nature no longer appears "quintaesenciada"[31] as it does in the first

---

31. Juan Bautista Avalle-Arce, *La novela pastoril española* (Madrid,1959),77.

part of the novel. Felismena records her impression of the Lusitanian fields in this way : "Las mieses que por todo el campo parecían sembradas, muy cerca estavan de dar el desseado fruto y a esta causa, con la fertilidad de la tierra, estavan muy crecidos y, meneados de un templado viento, hazían unos verdes, claros y obscuros, cosa que a los ojos dava gran contento" (281). Montemayor's delineation of this tangible setting is "almost cinematographic," with repeated references to things actually seen. Felismena's visual experience is readily transmitted to the reader, who partakes fully in the character's description of the historical world.[32] The fertile fields of Selvagia's native Portugal are nourished "de rocío del soberano cielo y cultivados con industria de los habitadores . . . el gracioso verano tiene cuydado de ofrecerles el fruto de su trabajo y socorrelles a las necessidades de la vida humana" (40).

It has rightly been pointed out that modern readers are accustomed to associating the words pastoral and pastoralism with artificiality, stylization, simplification, idealization, convention, idyll, and romance.[33] Indeed, such associations are often legitimate responses to traditional pastoral literature. But *Diana,* like many later pastoral novels, reveals an art form that combines pastoral elements with the everyday experiences of the common-sense world. Montemayor's treatment of characters as men and women who join in the basic functions of life is in harmony with a long-established Spanish literary tradition which sees man not as an abstraction but as a living person.[34] This concern for the "humanized" man reaches new heights in the philosophy of Unamuno, who scorns the abstractions of man, to study only the concrete being, "el hombre de carne y amor, el hombre que nace y muere, el que come y bebe y juega y duerme."[35] This conception of life revolving around man shapes not

32. Carroll B. Johnson, "Montemayor's *Diana*: A Novel Pastoral," *Bulletin of Hispanic Studies* 48 (1971): 32.

33. Michael G. Squires, *The Pastoral Novel* (Charlottesville, Va., 1974), 2.

34. Werner Beinhauer, "El carácter español," cited by Antonio González, O.P., in *Evolution of the feeling for Nature in Spanish Lyric Poetry* (Santo Tomás, 1951), 1.

35. Miguel de Unamuno, *Del sentimiento trágico de la vida* (Buenos Aires, n.d.), 7.

only Spanish history, philosophy, politics, and social intercourse, but also Spanish art and literature.[36] Thus Belisa goes to the river to rinse her clothes (137), and in Book IV the nymphs and Felismena take a bath not to cool off but to wash themselves before dressing up. In the midst of the novel's idealistic setting and constant weeping, the shepherds and shepherdesses follow the natural rhythm of waking and sleeping (92, 161).

Some critics have felt that references to eating in the pastoral are only cursory, that the herdsmen in fact "do not eat at all."[37] Not so in *Diana*. References to eating are more than just passing ones.[38] The first mention of eating in *Diana* is in an interesting figure used when Montano implores Selvagia : "Comed ora a mí que os quiero / con salsa del que queréis" (57). This makes the shepherds and shepherdesses forget their lovelorn condition and laugh. While Felismena recounts the story of her life to the nymphs and to Selvagia, the shepherds, at the nymphs' request, go "a la aldea a buscar de comer porque ya era tarde y todos lo avían menester" (92-93). Belisa refers to her carrying food for the shepherds in the fields (137). As sunset approaches, Felicia exhorts her company in the palace to put an end to their lengthy discourse on love and to partake in dining: "será bien que nosotros lo demos [fin] a nuestra plática y nos vamos a mi aposento, que ya la cena pienso que nos está aguardando" (203). In her journey away from Felicia's palace Felismena sees "una choça de pastores que entre unas enzinas estava a la entrada de un bosque y, persuadida de la hambre, se fué hazia ella" (229). Then "descolgando Amarílida y Arsileo sendos çurrones, dieron de comer a Felismena de aquello que para sí

36. Antonio González, *Feeling for Nature,* 2.
37. Thomas Rosenmeyer, *Green Cabinet,* 140.
38. In her unpublished doctoral dissertation "Et in Arcadia ego: Studien zum Spanischen Schäferroman" (Universität zu Heidelberg, 1966), Annemarie Rahn-Gassert says: "Arkadien wird in der vorliegenden Untersuchung als eine solche dichterische Welt zwischen Wirklichkeit und Ideal, d.h. dem Mythos vom Goldenen Zeitalter, gefasst" (7). Among the requirements of "Wirklichkeit" are such necessities as sleep, which shows up in *Diana* from time to time, and at least rudimentary cleanliness, much less important than sleep; taken less casually than either sleep or cleanliness by Montemayor is the matter of food and eating.

tenían" (236). Later they ask her again to eat something, seeing that she must have come with no little need for it, and she decides to accept (288). Thomas Rosenmeyer has asserted that the food eaten in the pleasance typically includes milk and cheese.[39] In *Diana* there is actually a reference to milking cows to make "mantecas, natas y quesos" (150).

Within the social context of *Diana* it did not surprise the public of the time to find that in addition to carrying out their basic human functions, the shepherds of the novel also spent a considerable part of their life singing and playing musical instruments. Singing is an intrinsic part of shepherds' life; shepherds were, after all, "criaturas musicales"[40] by nature. As has been noted, solitude invites shepherds to sing about the toils and hardships of their work, to chant about the beauty of nature, or to utter hymns about people dear to them. The rich collection of traditional lyric poetry gathered by Dámaso Alonso and José Manuel Blecua offers numerous examples of pastoral poems that have a distinct relationship to the reality of medieval and Renaissance pastoral life.[41] López Estrada stresses that the reader of the time did not look upon pastoral works as solely the product of the literature of antiquity, but saw them rather as an echo of a lexicon, of shepherds and their songs and musical instruments, of rivers, mountains, and valleys well known to them.[42]

When the shepherds are not speaking of love or praising the beauty of their women, they should indulge, Sylvano tells us, in those activities "de que los pastores nos preciamos, como son tañér, cantar, luchar, jugar al cayado, baylar con las moças el domingo" (30). Their talent in these endeavors is such that we can well say of *Diana*'s shepherds what has been noted of Góngora's peasants in the *Soledades,* that their skill at singing, dancing, and playing musical

39. *Green Cabinet,* 140.
40. López Estrada, *Los libros de pastores,* 518.
41. Dámaso Alonso and José Manuel Blecua, *Antología de la poesía española: Lírica de tipo tradicional,* 2nd ed. (Madrid, 1964), 32 n. 64, 41 n. 80, 49 n. 104, 80 n. 221, 176 n. 406, 74 n. 175, 90 n. 221, 198 n. 446, 82 n. 205. The social background of these poems is discussed briefly by López Estrada, *Los libros de pastores,* 281–92.
42. López Estrada, *Los libros de pastores,* 293.

instruments shows "admirable artifice" and a distinct "degree of culture and civilization." It is all part of the novel's "sympathetic realism" that softens rural coarseness to make country life palatable to urban society.[43] The varied forms of merry-making described by Sylvano's words is reminiscent of the ingenuity of Golden Age Spaniards to satisfy their craving for any sort of rejoicing. Dance particularly was a "national passion"[44] of the time, and Cervantes, reflecting this passion, wrote in one of his plays : "No hay mujer española que no salga del vientre de su madre bayladora."[45] With dancing, to borrow an expression of Michael Squires, "we smell the fragrance of leisure and festivity,"[46] which echoes not only pastoral life but also courtly pastime.

In the Spanish Renaissance people danced everywhere, and everyone danced. At court and in aristocratic circles, records the literary historian Marcelin Defourneaux, "the pavan, the branle, and the allemande were danced to the sound of instruments; measured and formal, by the grandees and their ladies."[47] For this, Sylvano's description of the shepherds' pastimes is significant in terms of what it reveals. In Castiglione's *Courtier* we are told that pastoral entertainments are a "calculated strategy to reveal the cavalier in the most favorable light. Though in his own person the knight may not with propriety dance or wrestle with peasants, in a masquerade he can freely enact his natural grace . . . because masquerading carries with it a certain freedom and license, which among other things enables one to choose the role in which he feels most able . . . and to show a certain nonchalance in what does not matter: all of which adds much charm; as for a youth to dress as an old man, yet in loose attire so as to be able to show his vigor; or for a cavalier to dress as a rustic shepherd, or in some other costume, but astride a perfect

43. Michael J. Woods, *The Poet and the Natural World in the Age of Góngora* (London, 1978), 164, 108.

44. Marcelin Defourneaux, *Daily Life in Spain in the Golden Age,* trans. Newton Branch (New York, 1970), 128, 129.

45. *La gran sultana,* cited by Ludwig Pfandl, *Cultura y costumbres del pueblo español de los siglos XVI y XVII: Introducción al Siglo de Oro* (Barcelona, 1929), 250n.

46. Squires, *Pastoral Novel,* 119.

47. *Daily Life in Spain,* 129.

horse and gracefully attired in character."[48] Thus despite its artifice and idealization of life, the pastoral novel is not as false as it seems. *Diana*, in particular, is an authentic expression of Renaissance idealism, exalting the values of the individual and of human personality while delving into the inner makeup of man.

Although the pastoral novelist is intimately and genuinely acquainted with the rural world, "he is or has been urbanized."[49] Such is certainly the case with Jorge de Montemayor who, to the vitality and innocence of rural life, juxtaposes the grace and elegance of urban culture with all its verbal sophistication, polished manners, and refined sentiments. As Lawrence Lerner stresses, pastoral life is, after all, "the work of courtiers."[50] The literary process relates to social life above all through its verbal aspect.[51] The shepherds' litanies in praise of female beauty and the grandiloquent verses interpolated in the novel suggest that they were more proper for utterance in a palace than in a campestral setting. Similarly, the witty exchanges, charades, lyrical descriptions of nature, paraphrases, apostrophes, and hyperbole are clearly reminiscent of refined speech. This stylistic virtuosity is dictated, of course, by guidelines that set the tone of behavior and verbal communication of the shepherds and shepherdesses, under whose disguises are hidden courtly knights and ladies. The word, says António Cirurgião, always has a social function to discharge.[52] The word, spoken or sung, mirrors the character's awareness of the social demands placed on proper language. This awareness extends to the use of the written word, as when Felix, after preparing a letter for Celia, shows it to his servant Valerio (Felismena in disguise) and asks him: " ¿qué te parecen, Valerio, estas palabras?" and Valerio replies "paréceme . . . que se muestran en ellas tus obras" (116).

48. Baldesar Castiglione, *Book of the Courtier,* trans. Charles S. Singleton (New York, 1959), 103.

49. Squires, *Pastoral Novel*, 12.

50. Lawrence Lerner, *The Uses of Nostalgia: Studies in Pastoral Poetry* (London, 1972), 21.

51. J. Tynianov, "The Evolution of Literature," in *Sociology of Literature and Drama*, ed. Elisabeth Burns (Baltimore, 1973), 185.

52. António Cirurgião, "O papel da palavra na *Diana* de Jorge de Montemor," *Ocidente* 74 (1968): 175.

As Roland Barthes has emphasized, "the very form of the literary message has a specific relationship with history and with society."[53] Thus, as the art of speaking according to certain rules is itself reflective of *Diana*'s social reality, so is apprehension about the intricate and excessive preciosity of language. Felismena warns against the entrapments of stylistic sophistication: "Mira, Armia, muchos males se escusarían, muy grandes desdichos no vernían en efecto, si nosotras dexássemos de dar crédito a palabras bien ordenadas y a razones compuestas de coraçones libres, porque en ninguna cosa ellos muestran tanto serlo, como en saber dezir por orden un mal que quando es verdadero, no ay cosa más fuera della" (290). It seems indeed reasonable to relate such codes of language to sixteenth-century Spanish society, which, as Barthes would say, both produced and made use of them.[54]

A careful examination of the text and its symbolism yields much information about social sensibilities in the sixteenth century beyond those involved with the art of language. If we concur with the view that man's "style" determines his identity,[55] we can see clearly that not only the language but the manners, gestures, tastes, and affections of *Diana*'s people reveal courtly figures. Says Arsenio to Belisa: "otras vezes acechando / de noche te veo estar / con gracia muy singular / mil cantarcillos cantando / . . . otras vezes te veo yo / hablar con otras zagalas / todo es en fiestas y galas / en quien bien o mal bayló; / Fulano es çapateador / si te tocan en amor / échaslo luego en donayre" (144). In a courtly context propriety must always be observed. Thus the ideal pastoral world of Book I is disrupted by a realistic injection of propriety when Selvagia closes her story with the comment : "Luego a la hora, nos fuymos cada uno a su lugar porque no era cosa que a nuestra honestidad convenía, estar a horas sospechosas fuera dél" (58-59).

Contemporaries of *Diana* surely recognized the shepherds as paragons of courtliness: the shepherds and shepherdesses "se

---

53. Roland Barthes, "Literature as Rhetoric," in *Littérature et société: Problèmes de méthodologie en sociologie de la littérature* (Brussels, 1967), 34, cited in Burns, *Sociology of Literature and Drama,* 196-97.

54. Ibid., 35.

55. Cf. José M. Sánchez de Muniain, *Estética del paisaje natural* (Madrid, 1945), 60.

vinieron a ella [Diana] y la recibieron con mucha cortesía y ella a ellos" (245). Diana is "recebida con gran cortesía" (266) by Sylvano and Selvagia. When Selvagia comes upon Sireno and Sylvano, she "muy cortésmente los saludó" (36). As Arsileo joins the shepherdesses by the spring of the alders, "él se llegó donde estávamos sentadas," explains Belisa, "y nos saludó con todo el comedimiento possible y con toda la buena criança que se puede imaginar" (154). "Alanio . . . por usar de la cortesía que a tan grande amor como el de Ysmenia era devida . . . determinó de acompañarla, como lo hizo" (46). Ysmenia's aristocratic background is betrayed by a reference to her "hermosa y delicada mano" (42). Filemón is described as a shepherd of "muy gentil disposición y arte" (259).

Montemayor's lovers "instinctively display themselves to others; their pride in their natural emotions is inseparable from a social context."[56] Although the cult of touch was greatly attenuated in Spanish amatory poetry[57] and sentimental prose, in Montemayor the embrace and even the kiss are occasionally witnessed. The inevitability of this granting of something more tangible than "mercy" or "pity" was perfectly recognized by the great theoretician of love, Mario Equicola.[58] Diana and Sireno embrace for the first and last time before his departure from Spain (87). Ysmenia takes Selvagia by the hand (43), and they take leave of one another with an embrace (46). The Portuguese shepherdesses receive Felismena "con muy estrechos abraços" (286). When the nymphs accompanying the shepherds arrive back at Felicia's palace they are embraced with "muy gran contento" by the other nymphs (163). "Y Felismena abraçando a cada una por sí, se partió por el camino donde la guiaron" (229). Henry Fielding once wrote, "I describe not men, but manners; not an individual, but a species."[59] These could just as well be words of Montemayor, who delves into every part of courtly behavior, including the kissing of hands, an expression of social refinement frequently found in *Diana*. Selvagia writes to

56. T. Anthony Perry, "Ideal Love and Human Reality in *La Diana*," *PMLA* 84 (1969): 230.

57. Otis H. Green, "Courtly Love in the Spanish *Cancioneros*," *PMLA* 64 (1949): 272.

58. Cited in ibid., 273.

59. Henry Fielding, *Joseph Andrews* (1742), ed. Martin C. Battestin (Middletown, Conn., 1967), 39.

Ysmenia "te beso las manos" (49), Valerio (Felismena) greets Celia with a hand kiss (118), and again Felismena kisses Celia's hand as she takes leave of her (121). In gratitude Arsileo bestows numerous kisses on Felismena, the bearer of good news (237). Upon his reunion with Felismena, Felix takes her by the hands and kisses them "muchas vezes" (297). Shepherds and shepherdesses kiss Felicia's hands before entering the sumptuous palace of the wise lady (164). Referring to Felismena's desire to pay homage to Lady Felicia, the author notes, "La pastora le quiso besar las manos . . . ; Felicia no lo consintió, más antes la abraçó" (224).

Theocritus (Idyll 8.57-59) confirms for us that pastoral literature is really a "mirage."[60] Seen in that "mirage" are the nymphs. We know that nymphs (like shepherdesses) are but fantasies or fancies in pastoral works, "yet, even if they fail to represent particular women, they stand for the eternal feminine, or for a generality that is a reality as well."[61] This view is made plausible by the characterization given to their behavior, apparel, or manners in *Diana*. Not at all simple creatures of the woods, the nymphs in Montemayor's novel are urbane and fashionable, exhibiting the clothing and headdress typical of sixteenth-century ladies: "Venían vestidas de unas ropas blancas, labradas por encima de follajes de oro; sus cabellos, que los rayos del sol escurecían, rebueltos a la cabeça y tomados con sendos hilos de orientales perlas con que encima de la crystalina frente se hazía una lazada y en medio della estava una águila de oro que entre las uñas tenía un muy hermoso diamante" (71). The chaste nymphs behave more like courtly ladies than like mythological figures.[62] In Selvagia's episode nymphs dance in the Temple of Minerva (43) and, in accordance with their characterization as noble women, do not play rustic wind instruments, but only the harp and other stringed instruments (73). With few exceptions (e.g., Gonzalo de Berceo's *Duelo de la Virgen*) the harp had been in the Middle Ages and was now in the Renaissance one of a handful of instruments reserved for those of the highest musical education.[63] The nymphs' aristocratic

60. Cited by Rosenmeyer, *Green Cabinet,* 230.
61. Renato Poggioli, *The Oaten Flute* (Cambridge, Mass., 1975), 229.
62. Mia I. Gerhardt, *La Pastorale: Essai d'analyse littéraire* (Assen, 1950), 179.
63. In Gonzalo de Berceo (*Duelo de la Virgen*) we read: "controbando

background is evidenced further by the surprise expressed by the nymph Dórida at seeing Felismena amidst "estos valles y bosques, apartados del concurso de la gente" (93). By these descriptions of courtly manners we are reminded, as Michael Squires points out, that the action of the pastoral novel often extends beyond the scope of the moral world, and that urban characters and urban life are introduced to heighten the sense of contrast and perspective.[64] From this it may be well to look, with Peter Marinelli, upon pastoral writing as "any literature which deals with the complexities of human life against a background of simplicity."[65]

It has been said that the pastoral "is always a mask, or even a masque, but there is always a living face, or a living person, beneath its mummery or pantomime,"[66] a person who conveys the human desire for pastoral peace and harmony. However, as John E. Lynen has remarked, "to yearn for the rustic life one must first know the great world from which it offers an escape,"[67] and that Montemayor knew well. Indeed, it seems that most characters of *Diana,* like those of many pastoral novels, are shepherds hardly at all. Their interest is love, a courtly interest of the author himself, and it is really only the occasion for poetry.[68] Although Cervantes expressed skepticism about the real identity of women mentioned in pastoral novels (*Don Quijote,* 1.25), his contemporary, the dramatist Lope de Vega, presents a different view based on historical material and reinforced by the belief that poets would instinctively employ their talents to immortalize their loved ones.[69] Seen in this light the amorous anecdotes of *Diana* are sentimental experiences of the author himself and possibly of others, friends and members of the royal court. This

cantares que non valian tres figas / tocando instrumentos cedras, rotas e gigas / cantaban los trufanes unas controbaduras" (cited by Adolfo Salazar, *La música en la sociedad española* [Mexico, 1942], 1: 249).

64. *Pastoral Novel,* 12.
65. Peter V. Marinelli, *Pastoral* (London, 1971), 3.
66. Poggioli, *Oaten Flute,* 229.
67. John F. Lynen, *The Pastoral Art of Robert Frost* (New Haven, 1964), 13.
68. Cf. Marinelli, *Pastoral,* 4.
69. Lope de Vega, *La Dorotea* (2.2) in *Colección de las obras sueltas, así en prosa, como en verso, de don Frey Lope Félix de Vega Carpio* (Madrid, 1777), 137.

is consistent with the Renaissance vogue for a literature of disguise and complex "plays" that would incite members of the court and the sophisticated reader to speculate on the identity of the participants. An admirable clue to the propensity for these social "games" is provided by the Italian humanist Girolamo Bargagli in his *Dialogo de' giuochi,*[70] where men and women amuse each other by "converting" themselves into shepherds or nymphs and then guessing who is who. It was a favorite trick of courtly poets in particular to masquerade as shepherds[71] or to pass their time reflecting philosophically on love, much as the shepherds of *Diana* do.[72]

The rich and varied pastoral onomastic in *Diana* is itself a reflection of the vogue in the Golden Age for taking on poetic pseudonyms,[73] often expressive of the human values of the time. The fusion of the real and the poetic, hinting at real people and events, is announced in the novel's "Argument" where the author classifies his work as a collection of "diversas hystorias, de casos que verdaderamente an sucedido, aunque van disfraçados debaxo de nombres y estilo pastoril" (7). Taking issue with the traditional interpretation of *Diana* as merely a product of the imagination, devoid of historical validity,[74] Mia I. Gerhardt has perceptively examined the various "casos de amor" discussed in *Diana* as representing the amorous feelings of Montemayor, according to which the novel becomes, for the French critic, a sentimental autobiography.[75] The relationship of *Diana* to specific events of Montemayor's life has been recorded since the early years of the seventeenth century by scores of prominent figures, among them Lope de Vega,[76] the Portuguese printer Lowrenço Craesbeek,[77] and the chronicler Faria y Sousa.[78]

70. Girolamo Bargagll, *Dialogo de' giuochi che nelle vegghie sanesi si usano di fare* (Venice, 1575), 45.

71. Albert Guérard, *Literature and Society* (New York, 1970), 60.

72. Scipione Bargagli, *I trattenimenti di . . . dove da vaghe donne e da giovani huomini rappresentati sono honesti, e diletteuoli giuochi* (Venice, 1591), 115-24.

73. López Estrada, *Los libros de pastores,* 494-97.

74. See, for example, Menéndez Pidal, *Orígenes de la novela,* 2: 185.

75. *La Pastorale,* 180.

76. *Dorotea,* 2.2.

77. In his dedication to the 1624 Lisbon edition of *Diana.*

78. In his commentary to Camõens's *Os Lusiadas* (Madrid, 1639), 2, col. 434.

Although no concrete documentation exists to support the theory that Sireno is Montemayor's alter ego, there is at least some evidence in favor of such a possibility. First, a stanza of the "Canción de Diana" (82–83) makes reference to what can well be interpreted as Montemayor's journey to England as part of the retinue escorting Philip II, "aquel gran pastor" (82), to England to meet his wife-to-be, Mary Tudor. The reference to the monarch as shepherd finds an interesting source in Themistius (*Oration* 1), in which he "characterizes the relation between ruler and ruled as one in which the ruler looks after his people in the manner of a shepherd or neatherd."[79] Another argument in favor of identifying Sireno with Montemayor stems from an exchange of letters between Sireno and Rosenio printed at the end of the *Cants d'amor* of the Valencian poet Auzías March (translated by Montemayor), where Sireno is identified as Montemayor, and where his beloved is called Diana. Perhaps the best evidence to support the contention that Sireno is a disguise for the author himself stems from the "Egloga tercera a la señora doña Isabel Osorio" found in the 1571 edition of Montemayor's *Cancionero*. Two of the characters of that eclogue, Diana and Marfida, betray, respectively, a relationship with Sireno and Lusitano, both adoptive poetical names for the same person: Montemayor.

Another character who is apparently a disguise of an actual entity is the shepherdess Diana herself. Contemporaries of Montemayor did not waver at all in considering Diana the disguise for a certain Ana, of Valencia de Don Juan, a town in the province of León. That relationship was stressed by, among others, Lope de Vega. In his leading play, *Dorotea,* reference is made to Diana as "una dama de Valencia de Don Juan, cerca de León." She and her river, the Esla, adds Lope, "se harán eternos por la pluma de Montemayor."[80] The existence of Diana's alter ego is affirmed too by Manuel de Faria y Sousa, a respected commentator on the important Portuguese poet Luis de Camões. Faria reports the interesting anecdote that during a visit to León by King Philip III and his wife Margaret in 1603, the king's majordomo, the Marquis of Navas, actually introduced Diana to the king and queen. Diana's baptismal name was Ana, Faria records, "una mujer ya entonces, al parecer, de algunos sesenta

79. Rosenmeyer, *Green Cabinet,* 99.   80. *La Dorotea,* 3.84.

años, en que todavía se miraban rastros do lo que había sido . . . aquella decantada belleza." The rulers were so pleased to have met such a "renombrada dama," and so impressed by her "gracia y discreción" that they bestowed scores of gifts on her.[81] These references to the identity of Diana find support in the writings of the seventeenth-century monk Jerónimo de Sepúlveda, who relates that the shepherdess in Montemayor's novel was in effect a woman from Valencia de Don Juan, a very able lady of the court, well spoken and the richest landholder of her town.[82] Narciso Alonso Cortés has advanced interesting possibilities of associating yet another character of the novel, Argasto (138), with a historical figure, the Marquis of Astorga, on the strength of the anagram "Argasto." Similarly, the nymph mentioned as related to Dórida, Cynthia, and Polydora (93) is seen as a disguise for the Countess of Lemos.[83]

Contrary to the skeptical view expressed by Cervantes' dog-protagonist Berganza that there can be no truth in the lives of literary shepherds,[84] *Diana* relates several of its pastoral characters to historical figures of the time, linking many of the deeds depicted in the novel with events that took place in the author's time. Not surprisingly, Valbuena Prat affirms that *Diana* is "el recuerdo de una aventura arrancada de la realidad,"[85] a product of the author's experience in and reflection on courtly life.

As a keen observer of the courtly world around him, Montemayor vividly sketches life at court with all its charm and intrigue. The pages of Felismena's tale are filled with references to gallantries and amorous encounters and the turmoil of courtiers, pages, and ser-

81. Manuel de Faria y Souoa, *Lusiadus de Luis de Camõens, Príncipe de los poetas de España* (Madrid, 1639), 2, col. 434, and note on octava 102 of song IV. See also Eustaquio Fernández de Navarrete, *Bosquejo histórico sobre la novela española*, in *Biblioteca de Autores Españoles*, 33; xxvii, note.

82. Jerónimo de Sepúlveda, "Sucesos del reinado de Felipe III," in Julián Zarco Cuevas, ed., *Documentos para la Historia del Monasterio de El Escorial* (Madrid, 1924), iv.

83. N. Alonso Cortés, "Sobre Montemayor y la *Diana*," *Artículos histórico-literarios* (Valladolid, 1935), 136.

84. Miguel de Cervantes, *The Dogs' Colloquy*, in *The Deceitful Marriage and Other Exemplary Novels*, trans. Walter Starkie (New York, 1963), 32.

85. Angel Valbuena Prat, *Historia de la literatura española* (Barcelona, 1968), 1: 756.

vants. Her characterization as intelligent, adroit, influential, and courageous is a distinct reminiscence of socially elevated women of the Renaissance portrayed as astute, intrepid, and heroic by chroniclers and artists of the time such as Benedetto da Cesena, Castiglione, Boiardo, and Ludovico Ariosto. Felismena's vicissitudes begin in Soldina (Seville), a city abounding in tournaments, music by night, lofty songs, and lovers' letters (100). There she learns social graces and the arts befitting nobility. From this we have a reference to her sending forth her arrow with "fuerça y destreza" (90), a talent probably acquired from her brother, a soldier of no mean accomplishment (99).

In Soldina, Felismena meets Felix and is courted by him with tourneys and jousts (295). When Felix is sent away by his father to the court of the great princess Augusta Caesarina (actually Princess Juana, daughter of Charles V), Felismena disguises herself as a man and goes in search of him. In her determination to remain undiscovered, Felismena seeks lodging at an inn that is "la más apartada de conversación que yo pude [encontrar]" (105). There she witnesses, in the street outside, a serenade by Felix and a group of musicians to the new lady in his life, Celia. The episode of Felismena taking on the identity of a man to gain entrance into the house of Felix can also be interpreted within a sociological context. As José María Díez Borque has noted, a woman disguised as a man provoked erotic pleasure in the Golden Age spectator[86] and, by extension, in the reader, and this device may well have been used by Montemayor not only as an element of plot but also as a way to entertain the public.

In the plaza outside the "gran palacio" Felismena finds "muchos cavalleros muy ricamente vestidos y en muy hermosos cavallos" (110). Among them is Felix, whose clothing, and that of his attendants, is minutely described. His retinue wear "una librea de un paño de color de cielo y faxas de terciopelo amarillo, bordadas por encima de cordoncillo de plata, las plumas azules y blancas y amarillas." Felix is dressed in the same colors, with white velvet hose embroidered and lined with gold and blue, a doublet of white satin

86. José María Díez Borque, *Sociología de la comedia española del siglo XVII* (Madrid, 1976), 47.

with tassels of gold, and a jerkin of white satin. His hat is set with golden stars, with a pearl in the middle of each, and he also wears blue, yellow, and white feathers. His horse is furnished in blue set with gold and seed pearls. His rapier and dagger, with engraved hilts and pommels of beaten gold, are in embroidered hangers. The only departure from this scheme is his short black velvet cloak, but that is edged with gold lace, hung with buttons of gold and pearl, and lined with blue satin. The servant Fabio, who is watching with Felismena/ Valerio, explains that Don Felix loves and serves a lady of that city and therefore wears a blue uniform, "que es color de cielo y lo blanco, amarillo, que son colores de la misma dama" (112). The colors are those of Lady Celia and are highly symbolic: white for her innocence "estava determinada de no querer bien a quien a dexado otra por mí" (119), and yellow for her jealousy.

In the love triangle of Felix, Felismena, and Celia the pastoral context vanishes completely. We are reduced here to what Menéndez Pelayo rightly calls a series of "escenas de palacio"[87] typical of courtly novels. The characters are ladies and gentlemen of the court; the action involves love, intrigue, and jealousy, elaborated by music in the streets and impassioned letters; the decor and ornamentation of the dressing rooms, rich clothing, tournaments, and emblems are all described with a profusion of elegant detail.[88] In Felicia's palace Felismena is dressed with clothing of a materially rich civilization: "una ropa y basquiña de fina grana, recamada de oro de cañutillo de aljófar y una cuera y mangas de tela de plata emprensada. En la basquiña y ropa, avía sembrados a trechos unos plumages de oro en las puntas de los quales avía muy gruessas perlas" (172). Even her hair is tied with an "escofion de redezilla de oro muy subtil, y en cada lazo de la red, assentado con gran artificio, un finíssimo rubí" (172). This array of opulent clothing and precious stones provokes a distinct sensation of awe.

The ostentatious and profuse ornamentation with which the nymphs at Felicia's palace adorn the head and neck of Felismena is an important reflection of a Renaissance vogue for gems and

87. Menéndez Pelayo, *Orígenes de la novela,* 2: 267.
88. Cf. Maxime Chevalier, "La *Diana* de Montemayor y su público en la España del siglo XVI," in *Creación y público en la literatura española,* ed. J.F. Botrel y S. Salaün (Madrid, 1974), 48.

pendants. In his perceptive study of the elegant jewelry displayed by Felismena, Francisco Márquez Villanueva has singled out the headdress made of a network of gold and rubies, and the earrings with pendants of emeralds in the form of two little ships with shrouds and tackling of sapphires, as being particularly characteristic of the time.[89] The detail and refined sensibility manifested in the description of Felismena's jewels reveals what has been called "un ojo fotográfico de conocedor profesional"[90] of precious stones, a fact made plausible by the report that Montemayor's father was a silversmith.[91] Furthermore the elaborately cut stones (diamonds, sapphires, rubies, and emeralds) are all sketched with words common to the old lapidary tradition and to that iconological language so prized by the humanists of the time.[92]

Diana's social and historical reality is eminently reflected in the description of Felicia's palace, a structure that represents "the zenith of high Renaissance artistic sensitivity, the epitome of artifice and creativity."[93] The exquisite study of the palace, also known as the Temple of Diana, done by Gustavo Correa points up the fact that architecturally the structure is "una construcción romana de suntuosa esplendidez, si bien se mezclan a sus líneas clásicas elementos preciosistas, exóticos y decorativos que son característicos de las visiones de ultramundo."[94]

From afar the palace has a luminous "aire de mitológica sobrenaturalidad."[95] In the middle of green and tall trees there appears to

89. Francisco Márqez Villanueva, "Los joyeles de Felismena," *Revue de littérature comparée* 52 (1978): 267-68. Cf. G. de Tervarent, *Atributs et symboles dans l'art profane, 1450-1600* (Geneva, 1958), cols. 281-82, cited by Márquez Villanueva, "Los joyeles," 270 n. 18.

90. Márquez Villanueva, "Los joyeles," 269.

91. This information is given by the Sevillian poet Juan de Alcalá; see J. López Toro, "El poeta sevillano Juan de Alcalá," *Archivo Hispalense* 14 (1951): 6.

92. Márquez Villanueva, "Los joyeles," 269.

93. Barbara J. Mujica, "The Wizard in the Spanish Pastoral Novel," in *Homenaje a Humberto Piñera,* ed. Wayne Finke and Enrique Ledesma (Madrid, 1979), 181.

94. Gustavo Correa, "El templo de Diana en la novela de Jorge de Montemayor," *Thesaurus* 16 (1961): 66.

95. Ibid.

the shepherds' sight "una gran casa de tan altos y sobervios edificios
que ponían gran contentamiento a los que los miravan porque los
chapiletes que por encima de los árboles sobrepujavan, davan de sí
tan gran resplandor que parecían hechos de un finísimo cristal"
(163). A close-up of the building reveals a tangible reality, however.
A huge square in front of the palace is checkered with black marble
and alabaster slabs. At its center stands a jasper and marble fountain
resting on four huge bronze lions. In the fountain four nymphs made
of white marble hold Roman-style vases with lions' faces from whose
mouths water spouts. The main portal is made of marble while the
doors are of cedar.

The sense of opulence is reinforced by the reaction of the wayfaring shepherds as they enter an inner chamber of the great hall of
the palace : "Según su riqueza," writes Montemayor, "les pareció
que todo lo que avían visto era ayre en su comparación" (178). The
triumph of art over nature is everywhere evident. In the back of the
palace is a large courtyard with arches and columns made of jasper,
their bases and capitals of alabaster with gilded foliage in the Roman
style; the walls are mosaic, the columns set on copper lions, lynxes,
and tigers which are so realistic that they "parecían arremeter a los
que allí entravan." In the middle of the patio "avía un padrón
ochavado de bronço tan alto como diez codos, encima del qual
estava armado de todas armas a la manera antigua el fiero Marte."
On either side of this pillar stand statues of Greco-Roman heroes
and of old and contemporary famous men (173-74). The great hall
of the palace has a ceiling "todo de marfil," and walls of alabaster
carved with "muchas historias antiguas" (177). An inner court has
walls covered with fine gold and a floor of precious stones around
which stand many life-sized statues of noble ladies of Spain and
other nations. Among the statues is one of the goddess Diana "hecha
de metal Corinthio, con ropas de caçadora, engastadas por ellas
muchas piedras y perlas de grandíssimo valor" (178). Corinthian
metal, incidentally, is a fusion of gold, silver, and copper, highly
prized among the ancient Romans[96] and an object of great value in
the Renaissance.

The hand of man is everywhere present. "Las paredes, de alabastro y en ellas esculpidas muchas historias antiguas, tan al natural

---

96. See Pliny the Elder, *Natural History*, 34, 2.

que verdaderamente parecía que Lucretia [the Roman heroine who killed herself after being raped by Tarquinius Sextus] acabava allí de darse muerte" (177). The double arched windows have locks and hinges of silver. This beauty and artifice extend to the furnishings of the palace, where its "ricas mesas eran de fino cedro y los asientos de marfil con paños de brocado; muchas taças y copas hechas de diversa forma y todas de grandíssimo precio; las unas de vidrio artificiosamente labrado; otras, de fino crystal con los pies y asas de oro; otras, de plata y entre ellas engastadas piedras preciosas de grandíssimo valor" (166-67). Equally opulent is the apparel of the nymphs, who appear "vestidas de telillas blancas, muy delicadas, texidas con plata y oro sotilíssimamente, sus guirnaldas de flores sobre los dorados cabellos que sueltos trayan" (163).

It is indeed possible that the rich social context of *Diana* may be linked to the difficulty of the Hispanic in separating ideal living from actual life.[97] As Lelius in Petrarch's Latin epic *Africa* (3.138-262), composed in memory of Scipio Africanus, one of the most famous soldiers of ancient Rome, describes in detail the pose, costume, and attributes of each god and hero whose statues line a splendid hall, so Montemayor offers a vivid portrayal of the "great hall" and its contents in Felicia's palace. That sumptuous hall is lined with marble and alabaster sculptures of famed legendary and historical figures, "todos aquellos que por las armas acabaron grandes hechos" with inscriptions bearing their names "y las cosas en que cada uno más se avía señalado" (173). Prominent in this parade of famous men are Horace, Mucius Scaevola, and Alexander the Great, as well as such exemplary Spanish heroes as the Cid, Fernán González, famed count of Castile, Bernardo del Carpio, and Fernández de Córdoba, "El gran Capitán," the most famous general in the time of the Catholic kings. There also is the famed contemporary of Montemayor, don Luis de Vilanova, knight and count of distinction, who fought in France and Italy (173-79) and to whom *Diana* is dedicated.

As a whole, Felicia's palace evokes what has rightly been called "a mixture and recreation of experience and reading, of life and literature."[98] Minute descriptions of it, taking up most of Book IV,

97. Avalle-Arce, *La novela pastoril,* 94.
98. Juan Bautista Avalle-Arce, "The *Diana* of Montemayor: Tradition and Innovation," *PMLA* 74 (1959): 3.

evoke all the present and past glory of Spain and give credence to the view that pastoral novels are "books written to express the taste and sensibility of their time."[99] With this enumeration of famous heroes, bringing to mind Petrarch's *Trionfi*, the *Generaciones y semblanzas* of Fernán Pérez de Guzmán, and the *Claros varones de Castilla* by Hernando del Pulgar, Montemayor exalts the national spirit of Spain and paves the way for the epic celebration of illustrious Spanish women sung by Orpheus. These include Maria Coronel, a Castilian lady of the fourteenth century, founder of the convent of St. Inés in Seville, and the subject of several legends (178); Maria of Austria, first daughter of Charles V and Isabel of Portugal (181); and Maria of Aragon, daughter of Alonso Philip of Aragon, acclaimed as the most beautiful woman at the festivities for the wedding of Philip II to Isabel de Valois (185). Among others is Catalina of Aragon, eulogized for her goodness and lamented for her early death, whose tomb rests in the sylvan setting of Felicia's palace (192). Many of the women mentioned in Orpheus's song are noble ladies who graced the court in Montemayor's own lifetime.

Montemayor's treatment of Spanish noble ladies focuses first on their physical appearance, specifically on their beauty. Detecting and representing the beautiful was a universal goal of the Renaissance artist, in visual art as well as in literature, as Jacob Burckhardt has shown,[100] and Montemayor reflects his consciousness of this by citing beauty as a trait of these historical figures in virtually all of the poem's forty-three stanzas, at times twice and even three times in the same strophe. As physical beauty is stressed, so also are nobility, richness, and social conduct. Evoking power and opulence, the portraits of Queen Maria and Princess Juana depict them with crown and scepter (181). The two daughters of the Portuguese infante, Duarte, are portrayed in lustrous splendor with sleeves of gold and gold-brocaded skirts adorned with pearls and emeralds (191).

As distinction of birth and wealth ceased to confer any special privilege on the individual in the Renaissance, society judged men

99. Gerald Brennan, *The Literature of the Spanish People* (Cambridge, England, 1951), 168.

100. Jacob Burckhardt, *The Civilization of the Renaissance in Italy* (New York, 1958), 2: 293–302, 338–43.

and women by their personal qualities, among them "discreción." This quality is mentioned no less than ten times in the song of Orpheus alone as a virtue proper to the illustrious women eulogized in the poem. The demeanor of individuals, and all the higher forms of social intercourse in the Renaissance, served ends pursued with a deliberate and artistic purpose.[101] It should not surprise us, therefore, that, as an echo of characterization in the rest of the novel, "gracia" is given as an outstanding quality of most of the women cited in the poem. In this respect the song of Orpheus evokes the splendor of a beautiful, active, and ethically correct society. As the women are also eulogized for their honor and patriotic valor, the poem serves to give Book IV a distinctly noble and heroic dimension. Indeed, as Jules Marsan suggests, the amorous and heroic dimensions of *Diana* derive from Spain's own adventure with love and heroism.[102] Friedrich Schlegel in his time noted also that the literature of Spain, better than any other literature, conveyed its national aspirations and values.[103] The song of Orpheus evokes the elegant courtly world of the Renaissance, its feasts and tournaments, its flair for beauty and fame. Above all it evokes the concern for national pride and dignity which Montemayor had already manifested so zealously in his revealing letter to Diego Ramírez Pagán.[104]

After listening to Orpheus's music and song, the nymphs, together with the shepherds and shepherdesses, pass into the temple's garden in the midst of which is found a cemetery of virgins, nymphs, and ladies who succeeded in preserving "la castidad devida a la castíssima Diosa [Diana]" (191). Consonant with the elegance marking the temple itself, the tombs and the surrounding garden display a high degree of artifice and workmanship: "Estavan todos los sepulcros coronados de enredosa yedra; otros, de olorosos arrayanes; otros, de verde laurel. Demás desto, avía en el hermoso jardín muchas fuentes de Alabastro; otras, de mármol jaspeado y de

101. Ibid., 361.
102. Jules Marsan, *La Pastorale Dramatique en France* (Paris, 1905), 111.
103. Friedrich Schlegel, *Geschichte der alten u. neuen literatur* (Regensburg, 1911), 2: 73.
104. Francisco López Estrada, "La epístola de Jorge de Montemayor a Diego Ramírez Pagán," in *Estudios a Ramón Menéndez Pidal*, 6 (1956): 402.

metal, debaxo de parrales que por encima de artificiosos arcos estendían sus ramas; los Mhirtos hazían cuatro paredes almenadas; y por encima de las almenas, parecían muchas flores de jazmín, madreselva y otras, muy apazibles a la vista" (191). One tomb stands out above the others: "En medio del jardín estava una piedra negra, sobre quatro pilares de metal, y en medio della un sepulcro de jaspe que quatro nimphas de alabastro en las manos sostenían; en torno dél, estavan muchos blandones y candeleros de fina plata, muy bien labrados, y en ellos hachas blancas ardiendo; en torno de la capilla, avía algunos bultos de cavalleros, y damas, unos de metal, otros de alabastro, otros de mármol jaspeado, y de otras diferentes materias . . . Mostravan estas figuras tan gran tristeza en el rostro," the author tells us, "que la pusieron en el coraçon de la hermosa Felismena y de todos los que el sepulcro veyan" (191-92).

Then, looking very attentively at the base of the sepulchre, the visitors to the temple see a metal tablet, held by a figure of death, on which are inscribed the words:

> Aquí reposa doña Catalina
> de Aragón y Sarmiento, cuya fama
> al alto cielo llega y se avezina
> y desde el Bórea al Austro se derrama;
> matéla, siendo muerte tan aína
> por muchos que ella a muerto, siendo dama;
> acá está el cuerpo; el alma, allá en el cielo,
> que no la mereció gozar el suelo.
>
> [192]

The epitaph, like her tomb, is a monument to her great beauty, whose absence has plunged the harmony of the universe into flux.[105] The somber pronouncement dramatizes not only the beauty of Doña Catalina and the swiftness of death, but also spiritual victory over death, which can only take the body, not the soul, from a world that is not worthy of it. Standing atop the tomb is an eagle made of black marble, clutching in its claws a golden tablet on which is carved the following epigram:

105. Correa, "El templo de Diana," 71.

> Qual quedaría, ¡O, muerte!, el alto cielo
> sin el dorado Apolo y su Diana;
> sin hombre, ni animal, el baxo suelo;
> sin norte, el marinero en mar insana;
> sin flor ni yerva, el campo y sin consuelo;
> sin el rocío de aljófar, la mañana;
> assí quedó el valor, la hermosura,
> sin la que yaze en esta sepultura.

Lady Catalina's highly elaborate tomb (191-92) reveals the common trend from the sixteenth through the eighteenth centuries to render the burial place individual and to perpetuate the memory of the individual in that spot with effigies and tombstone plaques.

A social dimension is added to the novel by Felicia's "mechanical solution"[106] to the distraught emotional state of the shepherds. Rather than relying upon human powers to induce his characters to love, as Cervantes does in motivating Fernando to love Dorotea (*Quijote* 1.36), Montemayor employs the talents of the enchantress Felicia.[107] In Renaissance Spain, interest in incantations and other occult practices was promoted by Juan de Herrera, the architect of the Escorial, who was an authority on magic and also close to King Philip II, upon whom he exerted notable influence.[108] Felicia's magic water and the effect it produces remind us of the hypnotic water used by medieval and Renaissance alchemists. With her superior intellect and wisdom Felicia fits well into the mold of the Renaissance alchemists examined by Fernando Sánchez Dragó in his history of magic.[109] As for the philter, it is useful to note the parallel made by Gustavo Correa between the therapeutic value of the magic water and sleep (which induces forgetfulness), itself a

106. Johnson, "Montemayor's *Diana,*" 27.
107. A comparison made by Avalle-Arce in *La novela pastoril,* 68.
108. See René Taylor, "Architecture and Magic," in *Essays in the History of Architecture Presented to Rudolph Wittkower,* ed. D. Fraser *et al.* (London, 1967), 81-109.
109. Fernando Sánchez Dragó, *Gárgoris y Habidis: Una historia mágica de España* (Madrid, 1979) 1: 11-44.

treatment for various psychiatric disorders.[110] A medical justification for the philter has also been advanced by Carroll B. Johnson, who finds in Felicia's treatment a forecast of modern lysergic acid psychotherapy.[111] The action of the drug, as Johnson reports, quickly breaks down psychological processes and resistances needing months of verbal therapy to accomplish.

It has been properly noted that *Diana* is to be taken as "the story of a vision which illuminates common-sense experience by illustrating a set of values more or less accepted by the conservative social class."[112] In *Diana* the marriage of the characters, brought about by Felicia's philter, is related to a social need to sanctify and institutionalize the amorous relationships of individuals. Charles Aubrun has addressed himself to marriage in Golden Age drama, for example, as an "ineluctable" condition, inevitable within the social values of the time,[113] values to which Montemayor strictly adheres. Thus the shepherds' struggles, resolved by marriage, fulfill not only an increased audience demand for dramatic verisimilitude, but also an important sociological need. If we remember that shepherds "are passive and resigned beings and leave to others the duty of defending their rights,"[114] Felicia's role becomes particularly plausible. Her magical rite becomes what Jane Harrison would call a "re-presentation" or "re-doing" of life, always with "a practical end."[115] Since loyalty is "the basis of permanence in the social sphere,"[116] flux and disorder follow its failure, as in the case of Diana, who remains unhappy because of her disloyalty to Sireno. Felicia's magic draught promotes loyalty and social stability, giving credence to the view that if the novel in general "expresses an unrealizable desire for universality, it also expresses the fact that universals really exist, however disguised."[117]

110. "El templo de Diana," 75 n. 15.

111. Johnson, "Montemayor's *Diana*," 28.

112. Bromberg, *Three Pastoral Novels*, 72.

113. Charles V. Aubrun, *La comedia española* (Madrid, 1968), 95-96.

114. Poggioli, *Oaten Flute*, 27.

115. Jane Harrison, "From Ritual to Art," in Burns, *Sociology of Literature and Drama*, 323.

116. Bromberg, *Three Pastoral Novels*, 78.

117. Michel Zeraffa, *Fictions: The Novel and Social Reality* (New York, 1976), 95.

Doubtless *Diana* is a *roman à clef*. The author defines it as such in the Argument, Lope de Vega later confirms it, and it appears that King Philip III, Queen Margarita, and her courtiers interpreted the novel as a work hiding a meaning.[118] Similarly, as Maxime Chevalier observes, Parisian publishers of the sixteenth and seventeenth centuries announced in the titles, annotations, and advertisements of their editions of *Diana* the novel's varied hidden meanings.[119] This is not surprising, for as Michael Zeraffa notes, "the form and content of the novel—even the novel of fantasy—describes more closely the social phenomena than do those of other arts, except perhaps cinema; novels often seem bound up with particular moments in the history of society."[120] Appropriately, Francisco López Estrada recommends that *Diana* not be elevated above the existence of the author, but rather be placed within the very course of his life.[121]

Montemayor spent considerable time in the Netherlands, and his presence there is picked up by Jean Subirats, whose perceptive study charts new inroads into the novel's frame of disguise.[122] According to Subirats, the central episodes of *Diana* are to be related to festivals at the Château Ténébreux at Binche (August 22-31, 1549), held by order of the regent Mary of Hungary in honor of then-Prince Philip, feasts at which the elite of the Spanish nobility was present. Specifically, these feasts are identified, appearing in pastoral disguise, in Books IV and V of *Diana*: the powerful Felicia is Mary of Hungary and the nymphs are ladies of the Spanish court who disguised themselves as nymphs during the festivities. The disposition of Felicia's palace is typical of a Renaissance chateau, similar to the one at Binche, and Subirats also points out parallels between the interior of Felicia's palace, with its abundance of marble, jasper, alabaster, golden pillars, and double leafed windows, with the interior of the palace at Binche,[123] highly renowned for its

118. Menéndez Pelayo, *Orígenes de la novela,* 2: 248-49.
119. Chevalier, "La *Diana* de Montemayor," 45.
120. Michel Zeraffa, "The Novel as Literary Form and as Social Institution," in Burns, *Sociology of Literature and Drama,* 35.
121. López Estrada, "La epístola de Jorge de Montemayor a Diego Ramírez Pagán," 406.
122. Jean Subirats, "La *Diana* de Montemayor roman à clef," in *Études Ibériques et Latino-américaines* (Paris, 1967), 114.
123. Subirats, "La *Diana* de Montemayor," 108, 111. It should be pointed

magnificence. In his representation of Felicia's palace and the events that take place in it, it is indeed possible that Montemayor wished to immortalize the famous fêtes of Binche, to give the feasts a "halo of legend."[124]

Subirats's connection is made even more plausible by the documented report of another episode linking *Diana* to the feasts at Binche. Vicente Álvarez reports that a stunning event of these feasts was a dramatic performance by actors dressed as "wild men" who attempted to kidnap beautiful women,[125] dramatic representations symbolizing a force hostile to society,[126] like similar events in Book II of *Diana*. Furthermore, the stage for some of those fêtes was not without allegorical figures (e.g., knights of the sea, moon, stars, and death, the latter a knight dressed in black velvet), and magic flasks,[127] music, and dance. Felicia, we will remember, appears clothed in black velvet and she too makes use of a miraculous flask. Furthermore, the entertainment in her palace includes music and song.

In addition to depicting shepherds in conventional musical groupings in which they play rustic instruments, the evening fête in Felicia's palace represents them with the nymphs in sumptuous concerts which include lutes, harps, psalters, and other "heavenly instruments," a fact revealing the novel's level of disguise and its courtly context. Like several sixteenth-century booklets dealing with Italian court entertainment which list in detail the instruments that

---

out that this is also frequently the plan of castles and palaces found in chivalric and sentimental literature of the Middle Ages and early Renaissance. See Howard R. Patch, "El otro mundo en la literatura medieval seguido de un apéndice," in María Rosa Lida de Malkiel, *La visión de trasmundo en las literaturas hispánicas* (Mexico, 1956), 203-4.

124. Michelle Débax, *Lexique de la "Diana" de Jorge de Montemayor* (Toulouse, 1971), 1. xlîii.

125. Vicenta Álvarez, *Relation du beau voyage que fit aux Pays Bas, en 1548, le prince Philippe d'Espagne, Notre Seigneur,* trans. M.T. Dovillée (Brussels, 1964), 100, 105-6. To Maxime Chevalier goes the credit for relating the episode of the "salvajes" in *Diana* to the historical reference to the "wild men" in the feasts of Binche; see his "*La Diana* de Montemayor," 46.

126. Daniel Heartz, "Un divertissement de Palais pour Charles Quint à Binche," in *Fêtes et cérémonies au temps de Charles Quint,* ed. F. Rumeau (Paris, 1960), 338.

127. Daniel Devoto, "Folklore et politique au Château Ténébreux," in ibid., 311-28.

accompanied the singers of specific compositions,[128] this scene in
Diana makes specific reference to the evening's musical arrangements, all carried, with the exception of one bagpipe, with the so-
called "low sounding instruments," which are most appropriate for
song and dance in the "salas de las damas."[129] The rebec, an instrument much cultivated in the fifteenth century but virtually absent
from the Florentine *intermedii* of the sixteenth century,[130] appears
elsewhere in *Diana* with vigor, and is also present at the festivity in
Felicia's palace, suggestive of its importance in the courtly musical
life of sixteenth-century Spain. Interestingly, of the twenty-three
instruments listed in the inventory of musical instruments in the
royal orchestra of Charles V and Philip II,[131] twelve are mentioned
in *Diana* and four are played by the shepherds and nymphs in
Felicia's palace. Here, as in the episodes related to Felismena's life
at court, music takes on a function of social realism that reminds us
of the early Italian and Spanish popular drama (e.g., Francesco
Cherea, *Egloga pastoral,* 1508; Angelo Beolco, *Pastorale,* 1520).

Whether or not the historical source of Felicia's palace and of
the events that take place in it can be positively documented, the
point remains that the whole episode bears social significance for its
portrayal of a learned and materially rich civilization, a civilization
of courtly men and women who walk the pages of *Diana* disguised as
shepherds and shepherdesses. A clue that the characters of *Diana* are
only shepherds in disguise is provided by the nymph Polydora, who
addresses a group of them with : "Desamados pastores, si es lícito
llamaros el nombre que a vuestro pesar la fortuna os a puesto, el
remedio de vuestro mal está en manos de la discreta Felicia, a la
qual dió naturaleza lo que a nosotros ha negado" (129). Fortune has
forced them to leave the court and retreat to the bucolic world,
where they can best analyze their sentiments and explore the nature

128. Howard Mayer Brown, *Sixteenth Century Instrumentation: The
Music for the Florentine Intermedii* (New York: American Institute of Musi-
cology, 1973), 12.

129. Adolfo Salazar, *La música en Cervantes y otros ensayos* (Madrid,
1961), 1: 251.

130. Brown, *Sixteenth Century Instrumentation,* 49.

131. Higinio Anglés, *La música en la corte de Carlos V* (Barcelona, 1944),
12 ff.

of love. The role-playing of the shepherds is illustrated further by the scene at the Temple of Minerva, where, before entering, the shepherdesses don their "serviles y baxos paños" and put on "de los mejores que teníamos" (41). Not only are the real members of society merely disguised as shepherds, they also recognize each other from their roles in the common-sense world. This is evidenced by the reaction of Felismena upon seeing Arsileo on her way to Portugal. "Arsileo," she exclaims, "más sé de ti de lo que te piensas, aunque estés en trage de pastor, muy fuera de como yo te vi quando en la academia Salmantina estudiavas" (236). In real life Felismena and Arsileo apparently moved in the same social milieu.

In Portugal, Felismena comes to her native region near Coimbra, a place that also evokes the urban reality of the novel :

> Pues, baxando la hermosa pastora por su camino abaxo, vino a dar en un bosque muy grande, de verdes alisos y azebuches assaz poblado, por en medio del qual vió muchas casas, tan sumptuosamente labradas que en gran admiración le pusieron. Y de súbito, fué a dar con los ojos en una muy hermosa ciudad que desde lo alto de una sierra que de frente estava, con sus hermosos edificios, venía hasta tocar con el muro en el caudaloso río que por medio del campo passava. Por encima del qual estava la más sumptuosa y admirable puente que en el universo se podía hallar. Las casas y edificios de aquella ciudad insigne eran tan altos, y con tan gran artificio labrados, que parecía aver la industria humana mostrado su poder. Entre ellos avía muchas torres y pirámides, que de altos se levantavan a las nuves. Los templos eran muchos y muy sumptuosos, las casas fuertes, los superbos muros, los bravos baluartes, davan gran lustre a la grande y antigua población, la cual desde allí se devisaba toda. [281]

With this description the buildings, monuments, and traditions of Montemayor's native Montemôr o velho are fondly and vividly recalled.

In Montemayor's novel, as in much of the pastoral genre, the principal subject matter is love. Since the days of Ovid, a function of literature has been to provide refined models for love and courtship, and the pastoral novel represents the transference of this function from poetry to prose. With all their idealistic contours, the characters and situations of *Diana* "convey a feeling about existence, a persistence and expansion of emotion."[132] As Sylvano reminds us of his love, revealing it makes it grow (31). Virtually every other character of the novel shares this sentiment, since a large portion of the work is a prolonged complaint over the grief caused by unrequited love. So pervading is the presence of love in *Diana* that it is not surprising that a leading critic concludes that the allegedly "artificial" pastoral background has "enabled the *Diana* to present, not false shepherds, but real lovers."[133] The amorous conflicts of pairs of shepherds in a chain of unrequited love situations give rise to sustained discussions on the theme of love, interpreted according to Neoplatonic doctrine, and the expression of a range of sentiments associated with the illusions and disillusions of love. The objective is the spiritualization of mundane love and the cultivation of a resigned suffering and melancholy as means of purifying the interior life.

Virtuous acts in *Diana* are seen as "titles of superiority: man takes pride in rising above his fellows and in being admired for it,"[134] a point reinforced by the words "los que sufren más, son los mejores" (167). The amorous context of the novel reflects cultural and social ideas of the time, shaped by the then-fashionable Neoplatonic theories of love. In its exposition of these theories *Diana* joins other great works of the Renaissance as a manual of ideal conduct in love, and reflects the *Zeitgeist* of the Renaissance: the best sentiments of the society of its time. It was the elegant novel par excellence, the manual of learned conversation between ladies and gentlemen of the sixteenth century.[135]

Aside from its value as a treatise of Neoplatonic philosophy, *Diana* reveals a variety of social and historical attitudes of its time. Ficino, we will recall, defines love as a seeking for beauty, by which he partly means spiritual luminosity as well as courtliness: beauty of

132. Perry, "Ideal Love," 227.

133. Bruce Wardropper, "The *Diana* of Montemayor: Revaluation and Interpretation," *Studies in Philology* 48 (1951): 144.

134. Perry, "Ideal Love," 230.

135. Menéndez Pelayo, *Orígenes de la novela*, 2: 267.

soul is a splendor born of "moeurs" or customs.[136] In contrast to this aristocratic conception of love, given also by Castiglione, in which love is a virtue associated with a hereditary past or with social position, love in *Diana* is a sentiment harbored in both the noble and the rustic. Thus at the end of Dórida's song the nymphs express astonishment at the news that a shepherdess like Diana could have been a "vaso donde amor tan encendido pudiesse caber" (87). Montemayor shows that love is not the exclusive asset of the courtier, of the nobleman, but that even he, a "salaried singer," can be molded by the amorous passion and with that transcend the social barrier placed before those lacking noble blood. Sylvano is taken aback by Felicia's discussion of nobility until she reassures him that it is innate (170). According to Felicia, true worth is found in one's own virtue, not in one's lineage: "tener el juyzio vivo, el pensamiento inclinado a cosas altas y otras virtudes que nacen con ellos mismos" (170). The concern with inner worth versus outer nobility, frequently manifested in *Diana*, was one of the most genuine social preoccupations of its time.

The brilliant but ephemeral success of the pastoral has been wrongly attributed to its "artificial character," to an art which, in the opinion of Luis Perrier, "is not inspired by the conscientious study of life."[137] On the contrary, to take up an expression of Northrop Frye, "poets are the children of concern,"[138] and Montemayor as poet and novelist displays a profound preoccupation with the social values of his time. A value of paramount importance in sixteenth-century Spain was honor. Diana's love for Sireno is so great that she would do for him all that her honor would permit: "quedando mi honrra a salvo, la qual te deve todo lo del mundo, no avría cosa en él, que por ti no hiziesse" (15). Similarly, in his rapport with Diana, Sireno avoids anything that would go against his lady's honor (20). When Diana marries Delio, a man whom she does not

136. Marsilio Ficino, *In Convivium Platonis sive de Amore,* ed. Raymond Marcel (Paris, 1956), 159.
137. José Luis Perrier, *A Short History of Spanish Literature* (New York, 1924), 44.
138. Northrup Frye, "The Social Context of Literary Criticism," in Burns, *Sociology of Literature and Drama,* 155.

love, she remains faithful to him. Thus, speaking of Diana, Selvagia tells Sireno, "Y después de casada, ¿qué pudo hazer por lo que tocava a su honra, sino olvidarte" (244). In spite of his uncouth and disagreeable nature Delio is still the guardian of her name and honor. Mindful of her reputation, Diana controls what must surely be the impulse of a vain desire to prove herself wanted still by Sireno and Sylvano and, albeit reluctantly, embraces her destiny and leaves her former suitors forever. Sireno and Sylvano remain oblivious to her departure, however, for they have been cured of their passion by Felicia's time-speeding magic water. "Change is the index of time's passing,"[139] and through the mutated feelings of impassioned shepherds and shepherdesses Montemayor depicts the toll of time on human life, but with honor intact.

Speaking to the wild men about to ravish the nymphs, Dórida is quick to assert her steadfastness in guarding their virtue : "Más fácilmente os dexaremos la vida en la mano que la honra" (89). Equally committed to guarding her reputation is Felismena, who writes to her daring admirer, "No tengas en tan poco, don Felis, mi honrra que con palabras fingidas, pienses perjudicalla" (103). As a woman of "qualidad," Felismena is keenly sensitive to her reputation and thus for "el débito que a mi honra devo" (99) she leaves home, disguises herself as a man, and embarks on a long journey in search of the man who once promised her his love. Belisa, the victim of the poignant tragedy recounted in Book III, belongs to a family of seminoble workers who zealously guard the purity of their household and lineage (136). Honor is uppermost for Belisa, too, as she contemplates a discreet way to reveal her love for Arsileo : "Toda aquella noche estuve pensando el modo que ternía en descubrille mi mal, de suerte que la vergüença no recibiesse daño, aunque quando éste no hallara, no me estorvara el de la muerte" (150).

The statue of the Cid, standing tall in Felicia's palace, displays the inscription "Soy el Cid, honra de España" (174). Similarly, two other epic heroes, Fernán González and Bernardo del Carpio, proclaim themselves as the "honra y prez de la Española silla" and the "honra y prez de los Christianos" (174), respectively. In his praise of famed Castilian women Orpheus himself chants above all of their

139. Jones, "Human Time," 142.

"gracia y honor" (180-90). Sentiments of honor and bravery, as displayed in Book VII by Felismena's rescue of Don Felix from three adversaries, reflect well the chivalric sentiments of sixteenth-century Spain.[140] No less sensitive to honor is Amarílida as she recounts to Felismena her tale of love with Filemón, saying at one point, "Y esto ya tú conoces si venía en mayor daño de mi honra que de tu contentamiento" (263). Felix's servant, Fabio, is seen as a man who prides himself as a descendant of the so-called "Cachopines de Laredo," people who put excessive value on their nobility and ancestry.[141]

Honor was often linked with loyalty to parental wishes, and in this respect the social framework of the novel is expanded by Diana's reference to filial duty. Obedience to her parents, she tells Sireno, provoked her inconstancy toward him and her marriage to another shepherd, Delio :"Moça me casó mi padre / de su obediencia forçada" (241). Sireno, on the other hand, argues that where true love reigns even the wishes of fathers and mothers must be ignored (273). Diana resolves the conflict between love and honor by following her parents' command to marry Delio, a solution often recorded in the history and literature of the Renaissance.[142] Like Diana, the shepherd Danteo succumbs to social pressures and is married against his will by his father. Just as Sireno blames Diana for allowing her life to be molded by her family, so the Portuguese girl Duarda blames Danteo for accepting his family's marital choice :"No trates de sus palabras," says Duarda to her friend Armia, "trata de sus obras que por ellas se ha de juzgar el pensamiento del que las haze" (290). Yet in the intricate story of confused lovers told by the shepherdess Selvagia, affections are altered and realtered not by parental will but by the fickleness of youthful love, which, as E.K. Chambers has suggested, makes the lover "at odds for the time with all established order of things, a rebel against the authority of parents, a rebel against friendship, a rebel against his own vows."[143]

140. See Hector Genouy, *L'"Arcadia" de Sidney dans ses rapports avec l'"Arcadia" de Sannazaro et la "Diana" de Montemayor* (Paris, 1928), 79.

141. Cervantes also recalls these pretentious individuals in *Quijote*, 1: 13; see Alonso Cortés, "Sobre Montemayor y la *Diana*," 70-75.

142. See H. Th. Oostendorp, *El conflicto entre el honor y el amor en la literatura española hasta el siglo XVII* (The Hague, 1962), 107-99.

In *Diana* woman's fickleness is the object of censure. Stemming from a current as old as humanity itself, this male complaint appeared in force in the Middle Ages, first in the French fabliaux, then in the *Roman de la Rose* by Jean de Meung, and then in Boccaccio, Martínez de Toledo, and scores of Renaissance writings. Writing about the "Querelle des femmes" in France, Abel Lefranc declares: "C'est, du reste, une vieille querelle, aussi ancienne que le monde, puisqu'elle commença á l'aurore de l'humanité, au moment où notre première mère tendit la pomme à notre premier père, et elle durera sans doute jusqu'á la fin des âges."[144] In an apparent imitation of the antifeminism expressed by Sannazzaro in Eclogue VIII of his *Arcadia,* Montemayor lodges his protest against woman in the following verses : "Mira el amor lo que ordena / que os viene a hazer a creer / cosas dichas por mujer / y escritas en el arena" (14). Although both Sireno and Sylvano are ostensibly favorable to women, both nevertheless berate women's fickleness, their unreliability, and their superficiality (37–38). The best illustration of this is Diana, who is reproached by Sireno for her misuse of love: " ¡O constancia, o firmeza, y quán pocas vezes hazéis assiento sobre coraçón de hembra! Que quanto más subjecta está a quereros, tanto más prompta para olvidaros" (27–28). This negative view of woman is not restricted to male characters. It is echoed by Felismena, herself a model of unbending love, as she admits to Arsileo that "no hay en la vida . . . cosa que en más se deva tener que la firmeza y más en coraçón de muger adonde las menos vezes suele hallarse" (236). A contrary opinion, but much more meaningful in sociological terms, is voiced by Selvagia, who comments, in an assertive tone that reminds us of the new spirit of the Renaissance woman: "Yo te digo, Sireno, que la causa porque las pastoras olvidamos no es otra sino la misma porque de vosotros somos olvidadas. Son cosas que el amor haze y deshaze, cosas que los tiempos y los lugares las mueven o les ponen silencio" (38). The implication of Selvagia's words is clear:

---

143. E.K. Chambers, ed., *A Midsummer Night's Dream,* quoted by T.P. Harrison, Jr., "Shakespeare and Montemayor's *Diana,*" *Texas University Studies in English* 6 (1926): 100.

144. Abel Lefranc, *Grands écrivains français de la Renaissance* (Paris, 1914), 253.

the behavior of woman is to be governed by the same rules as those affecting man.

In the Renaissance, writes Robert L. Hathaway, "the profeminist movement seemed eager to counter the . . . misogynist attacks with even more praise for womanhood,"[145] and with a concomitant stronger scorn for man. Accordingly Selvagia attacks men for their presumption in these words to Sireno: "Si [las mujeres] os hablan bien, pensáis que están muertas de amores; si no os hablan, creéis que de alteradas y fantásticas lo hazen; si el recogimiento que tienen no haze a vuestro propósito, tenéislo por ypocresía" (39). In Montemayor's novel, notes Bruce Wardropper, men misjudge women "and are called to task for it by a woman; the great originality of the *Diana* was that it gave men and women an opportunity to exchange points of view. Men for the first time were able to see themselves as women saw them."[146]

With the introduction of Selvagia, "a woman of flesh and blood and intellect—as well as beauty, the representation of women in the pastoral romances changes. They become strong characters, often stronger than men, and their presence leads to a more complete consideration of the problems of love"[147] and of other issues, as well. In her discussion with Sylvano over Diana's conduct, Selvagia emerges as an early defender of women's rights.[148] "Si Diana jamás se acordó de ti," Selvagia reprimandingly tells Sylvano, "¿cómo puedes tú quexarte de su olvido?" (37). Selvagia objects to women's inferior role in life (39). Against traditional beliefs, the nymph Cynthia teaches that absence does not make the heart grow fonder (202), and Felicia admits that time cannot heal all griefs (203).

The fact that in *Diana* the shepherdesses "act and talk far more than the shepherds"[149] is itself a reflection of the social prominence

145. Robert L. Hathaway, *Love in the Early Spanish Theatre* (Madrid, 1975), 15.

146. Wardropper, "The *Diana* of Montemayor," 142.

147. Evonne P. Buck, "The Renaissance Pastoral Romance: A Study of Genre and Theme in Sannazaro, Montemayor, Sidney and D'Urfé," Ph.D. diss., Univ. of Michigan, 1975, 61.

148. Mueller, "Montemayor's *Diana,*" 104.

149. Wardropper, "The *Diana* of Montemayor," 129.

of sixteenth-century upper-class women who, according to Jacob
Burckhardt, had come to stand "on a footing of perfect equality with
men,"[150] often taking a leading role in influencing events of the
time. It would then be difficult to concur with the view that in
Diana "women are granted an equality with men that the social
conventions of an urban setting would deny them"[151] Rather it is
the emancipation of Renaissance women and their prominent role in
the higher social circles that can explain, in part at least, why
Diana "is written more from the feminine viewpoint than from the
masculine."[152]

Some emancipated women in *Diana* bring forth a readily identifiable sociological trait, that of homosexuality. This may startle the
reader at first, but, properly understood, the pastoral has never
avoided what Eleanor Terry Lincoln has called "the realities of life,
nor has it been a picture of primitive innocence."[153] Thus, in the
dialogue between Selvagia and Ysmenia in the temple of Minerva,
one shepherdess asks the other: "¿Cómo puede ser, pastora, que
siendo vos tan hermosa, os enamoréis de otra que tanto le falta para
serlo, y más, siendo muger como vos? — ¡Hay, pastora! respondió
ella, que el amor que menos vezes se acaba es éste y el que más
consiente passar los hados sin que las bueltas de fortuna ni las
mudanças del tiempo les vayan a la mano" (42-43). Homosexuality
in *Diana* can well find an explanation in Freud, who has shown that
desires similar to those portrayed by many poets and artists in
pastoral form lie veiled and repressed in the mind of everyman.
"Expressed or represented, gratified or not, those yearnings," notes
Renato Poggioli, "represent only what one might call the normal
erotic impulses."[154] To be noted, however, is that the pastoral Eros
"stops short of perversion, it exalts a kind of love that may be in
conflict with the law of society but that is in agreement with the law
of nature. . . . At any rate, it rejects the obscene and the wicked,

150. Burckhardt, *Civilization of the Renaissance,* 389-95.
151. Wardropper, "Montemayor's *Diana,*" 129.
152. Ibid.
153. Eleanor Terry Lincoln, ed. *Pastoral and Romance: Modern Essays in
Criticism* (Englewood Cliffs, N.J., 1969), 3.
154. *Oaten Flute,* 61.

especially when man is led to them by a taste for blasphemy and iconoclasm."[155] Even in the Renaissance, and particularly in the Spanish Renaissance, culture and mores were so permeated with the ethos of Christianity as to preclude, in spite of the fervent imitation of the ancients, any characterization patterned after Virgil's homosexual character Corydon. Accordingly, in addition to the above-cited example of homosexuality in *Diana,* the novel offers an even less suggestive example of desire for a member of one's own sex in the following words of Felismena to Duarda: "No avría en el mundo, graciosa pastora, música más agradable para mí que vuestra vista y conversación" (288). However attenuated homosexual tendencies may be in *Diana,* their presence in the novel lends veracity to the view that the pastoral novelist "uses the genre—its potential for expressing complex attitudes toward human experience—rather than allowing the genre as traditionally conceived to dictate the form of his fiction."[156]

"Satire and pastoral were closely allied in the Renaissance partly through an etymological confusion of 'satyr' with 'satire' (in many minds the railing satyr occupied the same general region of the imagination as the shepherd whose simplicity penetrates courtly artifice), compounding an earlier confusion of 'satyr' with the Latin *satura* (satire)."[157] An important aspect of *Diana*'s satire and social reality is provided by Felix's servant, Fabio, who advises Felismena, disguised as a page with the assumed name of Valerio, to join in the service of his master, where she will be given food and drink, clothing, and even money to gamble (113). Fabio's practical sense extends to recognizing that Valerio, being a handsome young man, would have no problem at all attracting any number of young ladies to his side (113). In this context, Fabio suggests that his life, and that of other servants, is easy and pleasant. An old cleric's maid well known to him, Fabio notes, is even in a position to provide her friends with "pañizuelos y torreznos y vino de Sanct Martín" (113). Such characterization of the servant's life finds credibility in a comment made by a monk who ran an employment agency in Madrid's

155. Ibid., 62.
156. Ibid.
157. Squires, *Pastoral Novel,* 2.

Church of the Buen Suceso. To a servant for whom the agency had found work, the monk explained :"I have found you a soft job in a decent house; there are only a man and his wife; they offer sixteen reales a month and good food; and what's more, there's no need for you to go out of the house for it is Monsieur himself who does all the errands and the shopping." Furthermore, a sense of the "exclusive" position enjoyed by servants in Golden Age Spain is captured by the servant's reply: "Blow that! If the master is too mean to trust his servant, that's no house for me."[158] The author of *Día y noche en Madrid,* Francisco Santos, documents this and other instances of servants' arrogance, noting that with the shortage of domestic staff, servants showed themselves hard to please, and once they entered into someone's household they expected to live in precisely the way Montemayor's character describes.

Apropos of this question of servants, it does not seem unreasonable to find a suggestive sociological note in the burlesque reference made by Fabio to the "quite beautiful" maid at the service of an old canon. Relaxation of discipline and moral standards among clerics is often alluded to in literature and documented in history, as is shown in Marcelin Defourneaux's *Daily Life in Spain in the Golden Age,* where reference is made to priests having attractive maids who also served as concubines.[159] The fact that the priest's maid mentioned by Fabio wields so much power and influence can undoubtedly be explained in part by the favored position enjoyed by the servants of the time, but it can also be interpreted as a tribute to her ingenuity and very likely, too, to her intimate relationship with the priest.

Rosina, the young maid of Felismena, can also be related to social reality in satirical terms. Rosina is attacked by her mistress as a "traydora" with a "rostro [de] poca vergüença" (101). As in Lope de Vega's play *Amar, servir y esperar,* where the work of go-between is depicted, ironically, as "oficio de discretas,"[160] here too Rosina is called "discreta" (102) in the sense of "foxy," "wily." This trait is

158. Francisco Santos, *Día y noche en Madrid,* "Discurso X," in Defourneaux, *Daily Life in Spain,* 151.

159. Ibid., 107–12.

160. *Obras de Lope de Vega publicadas por la Real Academia Española* (Madrid, 1916–30), 1: 224.

basic among rogues and other characters of the underworld of the Golden Age, in which procuresses occupied a prominent role.[161] Such distinction of class and talent among various characters of *Diana* gives the novel an unmistakably realistic dimension.

A keen critic of gossip, Montemayor criticizes love in courtly circles where gossip and suspicion prevail (111).[162] He also points out the disadvantages of court life, with its pompousness, false flattery, and constant scrutiny of one's life, attacks the definition of nobility as a hereditary quality, and remarks on the instability of the courtier's life, always at the mercy of his master's whims. In depicting in such forceful terms the disadvantages of city and court, implicitly contrasting them to the purity of pastoral life, Montemayor is not merely following a well established convention; he is conveying his genuine personal sentiments about urban and courtly life. In a letter to his friend Jorge de Meneses he paints a picture of that world as a sea of discord, hatred, envy, lying, and murmurings.[163] Appropriately, Felismena joins the pastoral world to seek there a solution for her unfortunate love, a love scarred by the intrigues and snarls of urban society: a rich, high-born rival, a disloyal maid, and scheming pages. The urban world which Felismena temporarily leaves is plagued with the same complications and abuses that marred Renaissance society, as reported by Marcelin Defourneaux.[164]

Montemayor's sensitivity to social problems and historical events had already been well demonstrated in his essay *Los trabajos de los reyes*. There he comments critically on popular misconceptions regarding the life of royalty, who, far from enjoying a "paraíso terrenal plantado de deleytes,"[165] as is commonly thought, must constantly cope with the dangers of wars, enemies, jealousy, and hatred. Jealousy, like loneliness, violence, and evil, is a problem of

161. Juan Reglá, "La época de los tres primeros Austrias," in *Historia de España y América* (Barcelona, 1971), 144, 324.

162. Cf. Montemayor, *Los trabajos de los reyes*, 54.

163. Jorge de Montemayor, *Cancionero*, ed. 1571, 74v. This epistle is not found in the edition of 1554.

164. Defourneaux, *Daily Life in Spain*, 9-105, 212-28.

165. See F.J. Sánchez Cantón, "*Los trabajos de los reyes*, por Jorge de Montemayor," *Revista de Filología Española* 12 (1925): 45.

everyday existence that makes a marked presence in the pastoral setting of *Diana.*[166] It is an issue from Sireno's first song. Jealousy is present in the relationship between Ysmenia and Selvagia, and it is dramatized in the rivalry between Arsileo and Arsenio. Diana's husband, Delio, is notoriously jealous. Humanity is revealed when the normally benign Selvagia is gratified by her victory over Ysmenia, when Belisa plays off father against son, and when Diana, distressed with her own marriage, refuses to rejoice at the better fortune of others. Montemayor's insight into the passions, weaknesses, and aspirations of men and women makes him a forerunner of such artists as Francisco de Quevedo and Saavedra Fajardo. The Renaissance pastoral romance formed "a perfect vehicle for adjusting the actual and the ideal in life because it always placed the real and the ideal side-by-side. . . . Its setting was always dual: it included the actual world of human experience—whether stylized or naturalistically represented—within a kind of inner circle, a purified abstraction of that world, or 'Arcady.'"[167] While conveying the essential terms of the poetic pastoral setting, the timeless, universal, and idyllic nature, Montemayor also shows us sociohistorical elements that "are fused, not merely juxtaposed, with pastoral elements."[168] It has been rightly said that art has an inherent message, a communication which is either esthetic or social.[169] *Diana,* like the great works of Balzac, Dostoyevsky, and Proust, has both.[170]

166. Cf. Mujica, "Wizard in the Spanish Pastoral Novel," 267.

167. Walter R. Davis, "Masking in Arden," in *Pastoral and Romance: Modern Essays in Criticism,* ed. Eleanor Terry Lincoln (Englewood Cliffs, N.J., 1969), 71.

168. Perry, "Ideal Love," 227.

169. José Edmundo Clemente, *Los temas esenciales de la literatura* (Buenos Aires, 1959), 21.

170. See note 34, above.

Chapter Two

Sermonizing and the Practice of Christian Virtue

Montemayor's *Diana* must have betrayed the potential at least for some degree of moralization to the readers of the time, as is evidenced by the fact that Fray Bartolomé Ponce, the Cistercian monk from Aragon, considered *Diana* suitable for a version "a lo divino." *Diana* contains 68 mentions of God and 105 of Fortune; many of which, in contrast to the opinion expressed by Enrique Moreno Báez,[1] are indeed in harmony with the Christian concept of providence, and are ready testimony to the overriding spiritualism in Montemayor's novel. God is in the mind and words of virtually every character of the novel. "Plega a Dios que jamás me vea con más contento del que aora tengo" (37), says Sireno to Sylvano, remarking later to Selvagia: "Dios te dé el consuelo que para tan grave mal as menester" (39). As she writes to Ysmenia, Selvagia too calls on God for help: "Dios quiera que en algo te lo puedo servir" (49), repeating later in her song: "guárdeme Dios de olvidar / más que de ser olvidada" (58).

God is proclaimed as the source of beauty by Arsileo in his praise of Belisa: "Que vee qual os hizo Dios / y vee otra muy hermosa / parece que vee una cosa / que en algo quiso ser vos" (149). When Felismena awakens to the reality that Felix's love song is addressed to Celia and not to her, she confesses, "sabe Dios si quisiera más passar por la muerte" (107). Following the incident with the wild men, the nymph Dórida says to Felismena: " ¡Plega a Dios que algún tiempo la podamos satisfazer según que es nuestro desseo!" (92). Even Felismena's maid, Rosina, implores God: "Plega a Dios si mi intención a sido dalle enojo, que Dios me le dé el mayor que hija de madre aya tenido" (101).

In addition to conveying its spirituality through invocations to God, *Diana* makes patent its morality by a measure of sermonizing that includes simple proverbial expressions as well as messages of salvation based on free will. From popular collections of aphorisms come such comments as "no ay cosa más cierta que en las cosas súbitas encontrarse la lengua con lo que está en el coraçon" (46), "Toma exemplo en males agenos si quieres sobrellevar los tuyos" (59), and "nunca viene solo un mal" (85). Woman's inconstancy, the cause of shepherds' suffering, is a frequent source of moralizing: "A lo menos si hombre pone su descanso en manos de muger, primero se acabará la vida que con ella se acabe cosa que se espere recebille" (36).

Human helplessness before time and destiny is also reflected upon. Sireno reminds Selvagia: "Mas nadie haga cuenta sin la fortuna, ni fundamento sin considerar las mudanças de los tiempos" (239). Sireno's powerlessness is reported by the nymph Dórida: "Mas créeme ques muy en vano / según contino me siento / passarte por pensamiento / que pueda estar en mi mano / cosa que me dé contento" (83). Resignation in the face of hopelessness is conveyed by Armia and Duarda as they sing together: "Que avida sen esperança / ja não teme desenganos" (286).

Montemayor's characters reflect frequently on desire, love, and suffering: "Con lo que un hombre cansa, otro reposa / tras su desseo camina cada uno" (17); "Que el coraçón desusado / de sufrir pena o tormento / si no sobra entendimiento / qualquier pequeño cuydado / le cautiva el sufrimiento" (74). Belisa reminds the nymphs, "Mal que con el tiempo se cura, con poca dificultad puede sufrirse" (159-60). Sylvano comforts his friend Sireno with these words: "Tu mal me di, pastor, que el mal diziéndose / se passa a menos costa que callándolo / y la tristeza en fin va despidiéndose" (30). Regarding suffering, Selvagia instructs Sylvano thus: "Que no quieras mayor señal de ser el amor mucho o poco, la passión pequeña o grande, que oilla dezir al que la siente. Porque nunca passión bien sentida pudo ser bien manifestada con la lengua del que la padece" (68-69).

There is, too, a profound lesson to be derived from Selvagia's

---

1. *Los siete libros de la Diana,* ed. Enrique Moreno Báez (Madrid, 1976), xxviii.

recognition that the torment she must bear is a direct consequence of having surrendered her willpower to love: "Este mal en que me veo / yo lo meresco ¡ay, perdida! / pues vengo a poner la vida / en las manos del desseo" (60). The power of free will is conveyed by Sylvano's answer to a question posed by Sireno: " ¿Por ventura . . . está en su mano [la de Selvagia] el desengañarse?" "Sy," replies Sylvano, "porque no puedo yo creer que ay muger en la vida que tanto quiera que la fuerça del amor le estorve entender si es querida o no" (34-35).

It has rightly been said that, from a religious point of view, "the shepherd is the one disguise which is no disguise, since it stands for spiritual nudity,"[2] a state not affected by the senses, a condition that adds a quality of permanence to the life of man, and one which moves him closer to God. In a way that reminds us of the dynamic manner in which the "excellence and perfection" of pastoral life is discussed in the third colloquy of Antonio de Torquemada's *Coloquios satíricos, Diana* portrays its rustic characters as models of virtue. The propensity for the moral and instructive purpose that Montemayor exhibits in *Diana* may well stem, in part at least, from his service as singer and musician at the courts of Charles V and Philip II. It is probable that Montemayor there came into contact with individuals concerned about the religious turmoil of the Reformation and the prolonged Council of Trent.[3] Montemayor's didactic bent was revealed early in his writing career with the publication of a *Diálogo spiritual,* a primarily biblical work written in a vulgar tongue to provide an elementary introduction to the faith for those not able to read Latin. An acute observer of God's creation, and a patient and thorough explicator of the natural and theological symbolism of that creation, Montemayor stresses in *Diana,* as in the *Diálogo spiritual,* the supremacy of faith, hope, and charity, the three Christian virtues.

The pastoral, after all, writes Edward William Tayler, "is a form of meditation . . . on the complex virtues and vices of the author's

2. Bromberg, *Three Pastoral Novels,* 114.

3. Cf. Francisco López Estrada, "La Exposición moral sobre el salmo LXXXVI de Jorge de Montemayor," *Revista de Bibliografía Nacional* 5 (1944): 501.

audience."[4] The foremost virtue to be manifested in *Diana* is that of charity. This is seen in the manner in which the perpetually rejected Sylvano prefers to continue his suffering rather than to inflict a moment of displeasure on Diana: "una sola hora de tristeza no quisiera yo que por mi señora passara, aunque della se me siguieran a mí cien mil de alegría" (23). His charity is evident too as he continues to embrace his rival's friendship while accepting with kindness the favors shown by Diana to Sireno: "¿Pensar deves, Sireno, que te quería yo mal porque Dios te quería bien? ¿y que los favores que ella te hazía, eran parte para que yo te desamasse? Pues no era de tan baxos quilates mi fe, que no siguiesse a mi señora, no sólo en quererla, sino en querer todo lo que ella quisiesse. Pesarme de tu fatiga, no tienes porqué agradecérmelo; porque estoy tan hecho a pesares que aun de bienes míos me pesaría, quanto más de males agenos" (19). Sylvano's compassion for Sireno will endure to the very end of the novel (238). In fact, as has already been observed, in *Diana* "the characters' own growth is measured by their response to others' misfortunes."[5] Referring to Sylvano's charitable attitude toward his rival in love, the author reports: "Llegóse a él [Sireno] abraçándose los dos con muchas lágrimas, se bolvieron a sentar" (19).

For his part, Sireno, despite his rejection by Diana for another man, remains faithful to his beloved, as is seen by the respect and chivalric honor with which he continues to refer to her: "Nunca yo vea el remedio de mi mal si de Diana esperé, ni desseé cosa que contra su honrra fuesse y si por la imaginación me passava, era tanta su hermosura, su valor, su honestidad y la limpieza del amor que me tenía, que me quitavan del pensamiento qualquiera cosa que en daño de su bondad imaginasse" (20-21). Asked by Felicia what he would do if by chance Diana were now single and wanted to marry Sylvano, Sireno, cured of his passion, replies: "Yo mismo fuera el que tratara de concertallo" (225).

At the thought that her loved one, Alanio, would marry another woman, Selvagia introduces the following note of Christian charity: "Plega a Dios que ya que no fué mi ventura podelle gozar, que

4. *Nature and Art,* 56.
5. Mueller, "Montemayor's *Diana,*" 26.

con la nueva esposa se goze como yo desseo, que no será poco, porque el amor que yo le tengo no sufre menos sino dessealle todo el contento del mundo" (59). The complex love situation in which Alanio becomes enamored of Ysmenia, Ysmenia of Montano, Montano of Selvagia, and Selvagia of Alanio, is explored with a note of compassion by Selvagia, who, like the others, is a powerless victim of love. Despite the deceitful conduct of the execrable Ysmenia, Selvagia expresses genuine pity for her: "Una cosa me duele en estremo, y es ver que tienes mal de que no puedes quexarte, el qual da muy mayor pena a quien lo padece" (49). Selvagia's sympathetic nature is revealed when, following one of her songs, "las lágrimas de los pastores fueron tantas, especialmente las de la pastora Ysmenia que por fuerça me hizieron participar de su tristeza" (58). Selvagia's beloved Alanio evokes a further note of sympathy with a moving cry on the human condition: "Amor loco ¡ay, amor loco! / yo por vos y vos por otro" (57).

Charity also finds expression in the way in which rejected lovers temper their anger against their beloved. The true lover never wishes harm to the loved one, as Arsenio, for example, shows by his promise to Belisa: "Que un coraçón que en mi pecho / está ardiendo en fuego estraño / más temor tiene a tu daño / que respecto a su provecho" (145). There is nobility of heart, furthermore, in Arsenio's expressed desire to die rather than to see Belisa suffer at the hands of an unrequiting lover (145). Arsenio's son, Arsileo, shows kindness as he generously grants Felismena her request to rest awhile in the hut he shares with Amarilida: "Por cierto, pastora, no falta otra cosa para hazer lo que por vos es pedido, sino la posada ser tal como vos la merecéis, pero si desta manera soys servida, entrá que no avrá cosa que por serviros no se haga" (236). Asked for food by Felismena, Arsileo gives it to her "de muy buena gana" (236), while the Portuguese shepherdess Duarda tells her, "Mas lo que fuere parte del desseo, hallarse a en mí muy cumplidamente" (288). Arsileo himself is the recipient of benevolence. During his prolonged suffering and seclusion in a remote hut, he is repeatedly comforted by shepherdesses (237-38). Charity is expressed by Belisa as she reflects on the suffering brought upon her by the deaths of Arsenio and Arsileo. "¿Porqué, cruel Arsenio," she asks rhetorically, "no quesiste que yo participasse de dos muertes, que por estorvar la

que menos me dolía, diera yo cien mil vidas, si tantas tuviera?"
(193).

Though *Diana* may not depend upon a system of class exploita-
tion, notes Rachel Bromberg, "it does depend upon a system of class
advantages; the lower classes are transfigured by grace of the upper
classes, among whom charity is still a foremost virtue."[6] Felismena,
a member of the upper classes, is a good example of a noble lady
who exhibits charity. When she hears Arsileo, dressed as a shepherd,
complaining of his bad fortune, she ponders the situation in this
way: "No sería razón que la fortuna diesse contento ninguno a la
persona, que lo negasse a un pastor que también lo merece y lo a
menester. A lo menos, no partiré yo deste lugar, sin dársele tan
grande como lo recibirá con las nuevas de su pastora" (235). Realiz-
ing that her beloved Felix is in anguish for another woman, Felismena shows goodwill by wishing to offer her life to ensure his happiness: "Y por estorvar la menor cosa destas, diera yo cien mil de las
mías, si tantas tuviera" (123). Seeing the life of a man (who turns
out to be Felix) threatened by three knights, Felismena does not
hesitate to put hers in jeopardy in order to save him: "La pastora
Felismena que vió aquel cavallero en tan gran peligro y que si no le
socorriesse, no podría escapar con la vida, quiso poner la suya a
riesgo de perdella, por hazer lo que en aquel caso era obligado"
(294). After Felismena frees Felix from his assailants, he repents his
unfaithfulness and the two lovers go to the palace of the wise
Felicia, where they are joined in marriage. Only because of his repentance and his proclaimed devoted dedication to Felismena is
Felix allowed to enter into Felicia's palace. Felismena further
displays benevolence by her forgiveness of Felix for all the suffering
he has brought upon her (298-99). Even before that event Felismena shows charity when she is called upon to adjudicate between
the shepherdess Amarílida and her excessively jealous lover Phileno.
In that episode she advises the shepherdess not to be overly harsh
with him for common human flaws.

The importance of charity is reflected in the characterization of
Delia, Felismena's mother, a woman whose countless offerings to
God fulfill her wish to bear children: "Acaeció, pues, que como mi

6. *Three Pastoral Novels,* 59.

madre, aviendo muchos años que era casada, no tuviesse hijos, y a causa desto viviesse tan descontenta que no tuviesse un día de descanso, con lágrimas y sospiros cada hora importunava el cielo, y haziendo mil ofrendas y sacrificios, suplicava a Dios le diesse lo que tanto desseava, el qual fué servido, vistos sus continuos ruegos y oraciones" (97). It is worth noting also that the portrayal of Felismena's mother as a virtuous woman is enriched by her moral interpretation of the story dealing with the Judgment of Paris. In Renaissance art and literature, the classical tale can either adorn a tale or convey a moral lesson. The moral direction stems from the interpretation of this myth as "a trial of pleasure against virtue"[7] given by Athanaeus and Fulgentius, and repeated in the Renaissance by Ficino, who completed and refined the allegorical meaning suggested by Fulgentius:[8] the three rival goddesses, Juno, Pallas or Minerva, and Venus, represent respectively the life of action, the life of contemplation, and the life of pleasure. Paris's choice of Venus as the most beautiful of the deities became a cause of lively debate among sixteenth-century humanists as well as literary characters. Among the latter are Delia and Andronio, parents of Felismena in Montemayor's *Diana*. In Book II Delia contends that although it was written on the golden apple that it should be given "a la más hermosa" of the goddesses, this beauty "no se entendía corporal, sino del ánima" (98). This interpretation, which found ready acceptance among the composers of emblems and didactic lyrics of the Renaissance,[9] adds force to the overall moral current of *Diana*. Furthermore, the emphasis on the value of works, noted by Delia's "offerings," brings to mind a similar view implied in some of Montemayor's devotional poetry: that pious works are a necessary condition for justification.[10] In *Diana*, as in his spiritual verses,

7. Christine Rees, "Some Seventeenth-Century Versions of the Judgment of Paris," *Notes and Queries*, n.s. 24 (1977): 197.

8. The reference is cited by Hallet Smith, *Elizabethan Poetry* (Cambridge, Mass., 1952), 5.

9. Marsilio Ficino, "Epistolarum," *Opera* (Basle, 1576), lib. 10: 919-20.

10. See Geoffrey Whitney, *A Choice of Emblems, and other Devises* (Leyden, 1586); and idem, *A Handefull of Pleasant Delites* (1584); the latter provides "A Warning for Wooers, that they be not over hastie, nor deceived with womens beautie." See Rees, "Seventeenth-Century Versions," 198.

Montemayor shows himself keenly traditional in the importance which he attributes to works.

Montemayor, far from being the heterodox figure that Marcel Bataillon sees,[11] remains very much within the confines of Catholic orthodoxy. He promulgates themes and attitudes in accord with Catholic teaching. The importance of deeds, noted above, is also stressed by Duarda, who, speaking about Danteo, says, "No trates, Armia, de sus palabras, trata de sus obras que por ellas se ha de juzgar el pensamiento del que las haze" (290). In consonance with the Tridentine precepts of 1545-47, Felicia asserts the importance of good works, saying that "no ay cosa que sin ellos alcançar se pueda" (163). Like other characters before her, Felicia also prac-tices charity. In her palace, we are told, many persons, even those who do not deserve it, find a remedy for their anguish (126). Indeed, the imaginary world of Felicia's palace is transformed into a center of spiritual recollection and salvation. Before sending Felismena on her way to find Felix, Felicia assures her of everlasting assistance, with these words: "Y tened entendido que todas las vezes que mi ayuda y favor os fuera necessario, lo hallaréis sin que ayáis menester embiármelo a pedir" (222). Felicia also makes reference to charity by calling attention to numerous examples of those who gave up their lives for love of neighbor (198).

Felicia's priestesses, the nymphs, are equally sensitive to the needs of others. "De una cosa puedes estar certificada," says the nymph Dórida to Belisa, "y es que no avría remedio en la vida, para que la tuya no fuesse tan triste, que yo dexasse de dártele, si en mi mano fuesse" (135). Seeing that the disconsolate Belisa cannot stop her bitter weeping, the nymph Dórida comforts her with these words: "Cessen, hermosa Belisa, sus lágrimas, pues vees el poco remedio dellas; mira que dos ojos no bastan a llorar tan grave mal" (160). The nymphs share in the happiness of their fellow men; thus when the nymph Polydora comes upon Arsileo, for whose absence Belisa has grieved so pitifully, "el contento que desto recibió no se atrevía dallo a entender con palabras ni aun le parecía que podría hazer más que sentillo" (249). "Bien segura estoy," adds the nymph

---

11. Marcel Bataillon, *Une Source de Gil Vicente et de Montemór: La Méditation de Savonarole sur le Miserere* (Lisbon, 1936).

Polydora to Belisa, "que tú esso pienses de mí, pues sabes que me an dolido más que a ninguna persona que tú los ayas contado" (253).

Prudence, one of the virtues most highly acclaimed in Montemayor's essay *Carta de los trabajos de los reyes,*[12] is also stressed in *Diana* where, to extricate himself from the maze of fortune's ploys, man must rely not on blind ambition but rather on prudence: "nadie pudiera huir del engaño en que yo cay, si la fortuna de tan dificultoso laberinthio con el hilo de prudencia no le sacara" (45). Imprudence, on the other hand, brings suffering. Alfeo and Delio, one an evil sorcerer, the other an uncouth man who fails to practice self-restraint, are the cause of suffering for others.

Just as Montemayor extols the virtues of modesty, gentleness, humility, and particularly greatness of faith[13] in his *Exposición moral sobre el salmo LXXXVI del real profeta David,* so he stresses faith in *Diana.* This is seen when Duarda and Armia sing in unison their praise of the cardinal virtue: "A esperança acabara / a fe, me não deixara / . . . A vida se acabara / mas a fe não querera / fazerme esta sin razão" (286). As did medieval man, who lived in resigned submission to the will of God, shepherds and shepherdesses in *Diana* embrace their destiny to suffer with an equal degree of acquiescence, and they continue to forbear their passion deliberately until Felicia wills differently. Sylvano's forbearance in sustaining his unrequited love for Diana impresses Sireno to the point that he asks: "¿O acaso te a dado naturaleza tanto ánimo en ellas que no sólo baste para sufrir las tuyas, mas que aun ayudes a sobrellevar las agenas?" (20). The best example of forbearance is provided by the shepherdess Belisa. While searching for her beloved Arsileo, Belisa comes upon the false scene, concocted by the necromancer Alfeo, of Arsileo's death at the hands of his father. Arsenio in turn commits suicide for having killed his own son. Overcome with grief, Belisa flees the scene and, although convinced of his death, remains faithful to Arsileo. That faithfulness ultimately leads to their reunion and marriage by the wise Felicia.

12. Sánchez Cantón, "*Los trabajos de los reyes,*" 53.
13. López Estrada, "*La Exposición moral,*" 522.

The confidence expressed by Felicia that everything will work out for good is similar to the medieval belief in providence.[14] Felicia also preaches tolerance, even with respect to certain liberties taken during the heat of passion.[15] "Si el amor que el amador tiene a su dama," asserts Felicia, "aunque inflamado en desenfrenada afición, nace de la razón y del verdadero conocimiento y juyzio, que por solas sus virtudes la juzgue digna de ser amada; que este tal amor, a mi parecer y no me angaño, no es ilícito ni deshonesto, porque todo el amor desta manera no tira a otro fin, sino a querer la persona por ella misma, sin esperar otro interesse ni galardón de sus amores" (198).

Socially, "the disguise of shepherd equalizes everyone's rank so that his inner nature undergoes a test of excellence. The shepherd's dress means that the lover has denuded himself of externals to prove his worth from the beginning."[16] Sylvano, who takes pride in one's natural worth, is also the novel's foremost representation of hope. At one point in Book II Sylvano is seen with his flock in a thicket of myrtle trees, whose evergreen leaves symbolize hope as well as marital faith.[17] It is fitting and ironic that he should be cast in this particular setting, because of his singular longing for Diana and because of the shepherdess's inability to reciprocate his love due to her reluctantly faithful relationship with her husband Delio.

The principle of *aurea mediocritas,* extolled by both classical and Christian philosophers, is also praised in Montemayor's novel where Selvagia looks favorably on the way her countrymen practice moderation in all things, with their goal being that of "sustentar una vida quieta con suficiente medianía en las cosas que para passalla son

14. Ernst Cassirer, *The Individual and Cosmos in Renaissance Philosophy,* trans. and with an introduction by Mario Domandi (Philadelphia, 1963), 76.

15. John de Oliveira e Silva, "The *Arcadias* of Sir Philip Sidney in the context of the *Dianas* of Jorge de Montemayor and Gaspar Gil Polo: Religious Themes and the Language of Love" (Ph.D. diss., CUNY, 1977), 46.

16. Bromberg, *Three Pastoral Novels,* 114.

17. The myrtle is used by Titian in at least one of his paintings, the so-called *Allegory of Alfonso d'Avalos, Marchese del Vasto* (Louvre), as a symbol of marital faith. See Erwin Panofsky, *Problems in Titian* (New York, 1969), 127 and fig. 140.

menester" (40). Akin to moderation is temperance, a virtue suggested symbolically in *Diana* by the appearance of consistently
bridled horses,[18] the unbridled horse being "the most popular
Renaissance symbol of unbridled passion."[19] We are reminded of
this by the use of the uncurbed animal as a hieroglyphic sign for
Meretricia procacitas by Pierio Valeriano, who buttresses this un-
becoming characterization with citations ranging from Homer and
Virgil to Psalm 31.32.9.[20] Significantly, all the instances in which
bridled horses are referred to involve directly or indirectly Felismena, the champion of virtue. With the help of a friend who brings
her clothing and a horse, she, disguised as a man, goes in search of
Felix (105); on his way to court, Felix, elegantly dressed and with
richly attired attendants, appears upon a horse (112); Felix is attacked by three knights who leave their horses tied to nearby trees
(294); after being rescued by Felismena and redeemed from his misdirected passion by the magic draught given him by the nymph
Dórida, Felix, Felismena, and the nymphs mount the horses of the
dead knights and return to Lady Felicia's palace. Whether con-
sciously or not, Montemayor provides us throughout his novel with
bridled horses. As author of a book on heraldry,[21] and as one who
moved among the upper classes and royalty, Montemayor could not
have helped being knowledgeable about the symbols and signs that
were common information in his world. Bridled and controlled
horses are consistent with the controlled passion that Montemayor
shows us throughout *Diana*.

The biblical concept of sin and retribution, defended by Montemayor in his *Carta de los trabajos de los reyes*,[22] is echoed in *Diana*,
first when the wild men are killed by Felismena, and later when the
diabolical deeds of the necromancer Alfeo are overtaken by justice,
and the novel achieves a harmonious balance. Justice is particularly

18. Frederick D. Phillips called my attention to the symbolic value of the
bridled horses in *Diana*.
19. Panofsky, *Problems in Titian*, 138.
20. Ibid., 118.
21. Cited by Domingo García Perés, *Catálogo razonado biográfico y
bibliográfico de los autores portugueses que escribieron en castellano* (Madrid,
1890), 391.
22. Sánchez Cantón, "*Los trabajos de los reyes*," 54.

dramatized by the punishment bestowed upon the vain and inconstant Diana, who, unlike the other characters, is cast into a perpetual state of misery. Diana's vanity is clearly portrayed in the scene of Book I in which Sylvano recounts how in the early relationship between Sireno and Diana he had seen her combing her hair in front of a mirror held by Sireno (21). As Sireno contemplates Diana, she, rather than returning the lover's gaze, contemplates her own image.[23] The scene is rich in allegorical and moral significance. Reflected in the mirror, the beautiful shepherdess can only see vainglory, transience, and death, as does the woman in Titian's painting "Young Woman Doing Her Hair," probably executed between 1512 and 1515,[24] a picture conceivably known to Montemayor.

The mirror, notes Erwin Panofsky, "was the standard attribute not only of Prudence and Truth but also of Vanity, in the sense of being inordinately pleased with oneself as well as in the more terrible sense of the Preacher's 'Vanity of vanities; all is Vanity'; and it is not surprising that in the Renaissance it came to be associated with death."[25] Diana's repeated enchantment with the mirror "en que de cuando en cuando se mirava" (21), instead of with Sireno, betrays the tenuous quality of their relationship even in their early days together, thus anticipating her inconstancy and pointing up the frailty of human emotion. Regarding Diana's use of the mirror, it is well to remember too that in Dante's allegorical journey through purgatory, Virgil explains why the souls there are "thin" by giving an analogy from mythology based on form and its image in a mirror (*Purgatorio*, 25.22-27).

Diana is thus guilty of narcissism, the passion Rousseau two centuries later tried to channel back into the pastoral spectrum as a weakness to be shunned.[26] It is possible, however, that in his characterization of Diana, Montemayor wished to convey his concern with the moral dangers of idleness, a lesson perceived in a reference to the deceitful Ysmenia combing her golden hair by a brook (52). We

23. Ruth El Saffar, "Structural and Thematic Discontinuity in Montemayor's *Diana*," *Modern Language Notes* 86 (1971): 187.

24. See Panofsky, *Problems in Titian*, 91-92.

25. Ibid., 93.

26. Cf. Renato Poggioli, "The Pastoral of the Self," in *Daedalus* 88 (1959): 699.

recall that Felix is sent to the court of the great Princess Augusta Caesarina by his father with the comment that "no era justo que un cavallero moço y de linaje tan principal, gastasse la mocedad en casa de su padre, donde no se podían aprender sino los vicios de que la ociosidad es maestra" (104).

Regardless of whether it is idleness or lack of will that plunges Diana into pride and inconstancy, it seems she must be punished. As Sireno, now freed of his passion, argues, anyone who has made so many people grieve should suffer in return (244), particularly for having once sworn her unbending loyalty to him with the plea, "Y si el pensamento mío / en otra parte pusiere / suplico a Dios que si fuere / con mis ovejas al río / se seque quando me viere" (86). However, "Revenge, if admitted in the pastoral must be very ingeniously managed, or it will be intolerable."[27] Thomas Purney reminds us of an example of this found in one of Tasso's works in which a female warrior, opposed to her lover in arms, for his inconstancy shoots a dart at him yet wishes it may not strike him.[28] Similarly, despite his attitude that Diana should pay for her fickleness, Sireno wishes her well for the sake of his former love for her (246). He even tells Felicia, "El mismo bien le quiero [a Diana] que os quiero a vos y a otra qualquiera persona, que no me haya ofendido" (226). And to Diana herself Sireno finally says, "Plega a Dios, hermosa Diana, que siempre te dé tanto contento, quanto en algún tiempo me quitaste, que puesto caso que ya nuestros amores sean passados, las reliquias que en el alma me an quedado, bastan para dessearte yo todo el contentamiento possible" (246). As Renato Poggioli notes, in sectors of pastoral literature, as in Holy Scripture, "what is still possible and always necessary is retributive justice, which brings punishment to the guilty and the wicked."[29] For her impurity, Diana is denied access to Felicia's palace and, by extension, to the realization of happiness. At the end Diana, ignored by one suitor and forgotten by another, suffers as Sireno did at the beginning of the novel because of her marriage to Delio. She realizes at last that fickleness and

27. Thomas Purney, *A Full Enquiry into the True Nature of Pastoral* (London, 1971), 29.
28. Ibid.
29. *Oaten Flute,* 200.

inconstancy bring only suffering. Her lack of will has paved the way for her forced marriage to Delio, who now is tormenting her with his jealousy. Consequently she becomes increasingly melancholy because of the "triste sucesso de su camino" (265) and, significantly, turns into the unhappiest character of the novel. The now-envious Diana is further humiliated by having to acknowledge her disdainful behavior toward Sylvano, to whom she confesses, "Yo no lo miré bien en no quererte como tu amor me lo merecía" (267). The inconstant Diana is thus firmly castigated by the author, whose praise of humility and rejection of pride had already been sounded in his paraphrase of the 35th Psalm and in his long poem titled *Pasión de Christo.*[30]

30. *El cancionero del poeta George de Montemayor*, ed. Angel González Palencia (Madrid, 1932), 341, 143.

Chapter Three

Journey to Felicia
La Diana as Pilgrimage

The pilgrimage of life is a theme omnipresent in Spanish literature of the Golden Age.[1] In the literature of that time the theme took on several interpretations, including a wandering in exile from Paradise, a journey for the purpose of purging oneself of the sins incurred in one's disorderly life, and a movement away from urban society to a place of idyllic solitude by a disillusioned lover. Antonio Vilanova, in his study of the *peregrinatio* of the lovelorn youth in the pastoral poetry of Góngora, has found that it forms part of a tradition of Italian and Spanish Renaissance poetry. His findings point to the existence in literature of a fictional character who is a model of the errant lover, who is surfeited with the world and overcome with disillusionment, and who searches for consolation and oblivion in the solitude of nature. This character, who appears in an uninterrupted succession throughout the Renaissance until his presence as the protagonist of Góngora's *Soledades,* is the "peregrino de amor."[2] In Montemayor's *Diana* virtually every character is a pilgrim of love futilely seeking relief from his amorous torment in the realm of a seemingly sympathetic nature.

Much of *Diana* is set on the banks of the Esla river, which in its function, by plan or coincidence, brings to mind Dante's river Elsa, whose water dulls the mind (*Purgatorio,* 33.68). By the Esla, shepherds and shepherdesses in Montemayor's novel spend most of their time in idleness, commiserating with each other over their despair brought on by unrequited love. For all of them except Sylvano, the anguish is intensified by the memory of a love that once was. Thus, like men and women banished from a happy land, they languish as the biblical exiles did: "By the rivers of Babylon, there we sat down, yea, we wept, when we remembered Zion" (Psalm 137). Parenthetically, this psalm, known as *Super Flumina Babylonis,* was paraphrased by Montemayor.[3] In his adaptation of the biblical story of the Jews' defeat by the Babylonians and their subsequent bondage, Montemayor links the fate of the Jews to their loss of divine favor, in sharp contrast to the biblical origins.[4] It may well be that in *Diana* Montemayor wished to project an analogous plight of shepherds and shepherdesses suffering for having fallen out of grace with God's laws; hence the need for a spiritual pilgrimage to gain redemption.

Frustrated by love and tormented by suffering, the characters seek solace in the shade of the *aliso,* the alder tree, common to moist plains and once believed effective against rage and fury.[5] The peaceful quality of the tree complements well the tranquil setting of the river and meadows described in the novel. The tree thus becomes a symbol of that peaceful withdrawal that characterizes the entire pastoral tradition, a tradition often defined as a contrast between the simple, natural goodness of rural life and the vanity and ambition of the urban world.[6] The alder is a deceptive source of tranquillity, however, for although the tree provides the shepherds with an apparently soothing relief from the midday sun, it plunges them ever more deeply in the reflection of their anguish and the contemplation of misdirected goals.

1. Juergen Hahn, *The Origins of the Baroque Concepts of Peregrinatio* (Chapel Hill, N.C., 1973), 15. See Antonio Vilanova, "El peregrino andante en el *Persiles* de Cervantes," in *Boletín de la Real Academia de Buenas Letras de Barcelona* 22 (1949): 97–159; and his "El peregrino de amor en las *Soledades* de Góngora," *Estudios Dedicados a Menéndez Pidal* (Madrid, 1952), 3: 421-60.

2. Vilanova, "El peregrino de amor," 460; a work also cited by Juergen Hahn, *Baroque Concepts,* 63.

3. Jorge de Montemayor, *Segundo cancionero espiritual* (Antwerp, 1558), ff. 180r-188v.

4. Cf. Bryant L. Creel, "The Religious Poetry of Jorge de Montemayor" (Ph.D. diss., Unv. of California-Davis, 1978), 183-84.

5. *Diccionario de la Real Academia Española,* 17th ed. (Madrid, 1947), s.v. *aliso.*

6. See Frank Kermode's anthology, *English Pastoral Poetry: From the Beginnings to Marvel* (London, 1952), 14.

The shepherds' invariable encounters in the heat of the day sustain their grief and anxiety and threaten their spiritual well-being, for, as medieval rabbinical commentators of Psalm 90 explain, the heat of the sun renders man weaker than usual.[7] From antiquity to the Renaissance, noon was considered a time of danger. The psalmist David writes in Psalm 90.3-6: "deliver me from the snare of the hunters . . . from hostile attack and from the noon-day demon." And Richard of St. Victor in an interpretation of this psalm explains that demons come to us "when the heat and light of the day are at their greatest."[8] The shepherds' repeated gatherings in the heat of the day are invariably accompanied by memory-laden songs of love that cast the dutiful rustics in an ever-growing state of despair and amorous enslavement. The cruelty of the pangs of love that demand such an ever-flowing dedication with song and music, in turn bringing on more suffering, evokes the moving words of that famous psalm of exile (137.3): "For there our captors required of us songs." Continuous lament in dialogue or song can only lead the shepherds to spiritual death but for the miraculous intervention of the sage Lady Felicia.

The journey to the palace of the wise Felicia becomes the only viable pilgrimage for the novel's characters. The pilgrimage to the temple where Felicia will transform the discordance of the shepherds into harmony, their torment into happiness, is a perfecting, spiritualizing experience that paves the way for their ultimate reward. It is a pilgrimage marked by hardships, renunciation, charity, devotion, and temporary despair. The life of shepherds and shepherdesses quintessentially marked by amorous torment can be equated with the "ejecución de hazañas notables, . . . y en tal virtud adquiere una dimensión de heroicidad."[9] Understandably the shepherds proclaim that "los que sufren más son los mejores" (167), that "no es honra acabar pequeñas cosas" (168), and that love "está en unos tormentos

7. John Block Friedman, *Orpheus in the Middle Ages* (Cambridge, Mass., 1970), 162.
8. Ibid. The word *noon* comes from the Latin *nona,* meaning nine. The day used to be computed from sunup, and the ninth hour, noon, was three hours after midday.
9. Correa, "El templo de Diana," 72.

/ do los que penan más, son más contentos" (168), bringing to mind the biblical message that "The Lord disciplines him whom he loves, and chastises every son whom he receives" (Heb. 12.6).

The simple plot of Books I–III, in which several people (Sireno, Sylvano, Selvagia) start on a journey to improve their lot and are gradually joined by other travelers (Felismena and Belisa), belongs to folkloric literature and appears as early as the twelfth century poem of the *Pélérinage Renart.*[10] Montemayor, however, gives his novel a deeper allegorical meaning, making the journey of his characters a "pilgrimage in search of true love,"[11] a pilgrimage mounted by eschewing vice and embracing those virtues which I have discussed in the preceding chapter.

Disillusioned and distraught by amorous torment, the shepherds and shepherdesses wander aimlessly in the confused solitude of their *locus amoenus* until rescued from their meandering existence by three nymphs, Polydora, Cynthia, and Dórida, all priestesses of the wise Lady Felicia. According to ancient philosophy, the number three represents Time—past, present, and to come. Christianity used it to denote the eternity of God the Father, the ever-existent "I am."[12] The nymphs in *Diana* form a triad possibly bearing a significance often associated with the Three Graces as symbols of friendship and concord. Individually the nymphs also betray traits vested in each of the Three Graces: *Castitas-Pulchritudo-Amor,* as they are identified in a medal made by Niccolò Fiorentino on the occasion of the marriage of Giovanna degli Albizzi to Pico della Mirandola's pupil Lorenzo Tornabuoni.[13]

The supernatural and spiritual role of the nymph was stressed in the Renaissance by the Italian theoretician Antonio Minturno, who made a group of nymphs the principal protagonists of his semi-

10. *Le roman de Renart,* ed. Ernest Martin, 1 (Strasbourg, 1882): 265–78, cited by Avalle-Arce, *"Diana* of Montemayor," 2.

11. Frederick de Armas, "Las tres Dianas de Montemayor," *Lingüística y Educación: Actas del IV Congreso Internacional de la ALFAL* (Lima, 1978), 192.

12. Harold Bayley, *A New Light on the Renaissance Displayed in Contemporary Emblems* (London, 1909), 24.

13. See Panofsky, *Problems in Titian,* 136 and fig. 148.

pastoral work *L'amore innamorato,* published in Venice in 1559. As they are closest to the origin of the world, notes Minturno, they are also closest to the gods,[14] and thus they are the highest expression of harmony and order. *Diana*'s nymphs convey harmony and order by offering hope to the grieving shepherds and shepherdesses: "el remedio de vuestro mal está en manos de la discreta Felicia," says Polydora, "a la qual dió naturaleza lo que a nosotros a negado. Y pues véis lo que os importa yr a visitaria, pídoos de parte destas nimphas a quien este día tanto servicio avéis hecho, que no rehuséis nuestra compañía pues no de otra manera podéis recebir el premio de vuestro trabajo" (129). In this respect the nymphs themselves take on the role of pilgrims in a journey to save souls from perdition.[15]

In her intermediary role, the nymph Polydora reiterates to the newly found Belisa her call to the right path: "a lo menos podría mostrarte el camino por donde pudiesses algún poco aliviar tu pena. Y para esto te ruego que vengas en nuestra compañía, assí por que no es cosa justa que tan mal gastes la vida como porque adonde te llevaremos, podrás escoger la que quisieres y no avrá persona que estorvalla pueda" (160). The shepherds and shepherdesses acquiesce, and the nymphs, walking "con gran contentamiento . . . con su compañía" (131), guide them toward Felicia's palace. Their guiding role is dramatized by the episode, following the shepherd's encounter with Belisa, in which "llegaron a un espesso bosque y tan lleno de sylvestres y espessos árboles, que a no ser de las tres nimphas guiados, no pudieran dexar de perderse en él" (162).

While leading the shepherds to the palace of Lady Felicia, the nymphs continue to console their suffering companions: "no te desconsueles," says Polydora to Sireno, "que si tu dama tuviesse tan cerca el remedio de la mala vida que tiene, como tú de lo que ella te haze passar, no sería pequeño alivio para los desgustos y desabri-

---

14. Antonio Minturno, *L'Amore innamorato* (Venice, 1559), 4-5. See Francisco López Estrada, "*L'amore innamorato* de Minturno (1559) y su repercusión en la literatura pastoril española," in *Homenaje a Joaquín Casalduero,* ed. Rizel Pincus Sigele and Gonzalo Sobejano (Madrid, 1972), 315-24.

15. Cf. "Relation du voyage du frère Bieul," in *L'Extrême Orient au Moyen Age,* ed. Louis de Backer (Paris, 1877), 257.

mientos que yo sé que passa cada día" (130). Seeing that the disconsolate Belisa cannot stop her bitter weeping, the nymph Dórida soothes her with these words: "Cessen, hermosa Belisa, sus lágrimas, pues vees el poco remedio dellas; mira que dos ojos no bastan a llorar tan grave mal" (160). The concomitant and inspiring call to good deeds reminds us of Titian's painting *Sacred and Profane Love,* in which two Venuses "hold sway over the two shepherds of a world within which, as Ficino puts it, love is an 'innate and uniting force that drives the higher things to care for the lower ones, the equal things to some special communion with each other, and finally induces all lower things to turn toward the better and higher ones.'"[16]

The special function of the nymphs is also underscored symbolically by an explicit reference to their bathing in the nude. Erwin Panofsky reminds us that nudity in the Renaissance became "invested with an almost metaphysical halo" and came to be associated with a celestial Venus, who "leads us beyond sensory perception," in contrast to the terrestrial Venus who "rules the world of nature accessible to the eye and ear."[17] Botticelli observes this dichotomy in two famous paintings: the *Birth of Venus,* in which the celestial Venus is swept ashore on a shell, and the *Realm of Venus,* commonly known as *La Primavera,* "where the terrestrial Venus holds gentle sway over the flowering earth."[18] That *The Twin Venuses* is held to be the more appropriate title of Titian's *Sacred and Profane Love*[19] suggests the possible meaning inherent in the redeeming nymphs of *Diana,* carefully portrayed in their superior symbolic nudity, the only characters so represented in the novel with the exception of Felismena, the other great inspiring force of *Diana,* who bathes with them.

Novelistically, the association of Felismena with the nymphs comes about when she rescues the sylvan maidens from the clutches

16. The comment made by Oskar Kristeller, *The Philosophy of Marsilio Ficino,* 112, cited in Panofsky, *Problems in Titian,* 119.
17. *Problems in Titian,* 114.
18. Ibid.
19. Ibid., 115.

of three wild men intent on ravishing them (90). Significantly, the drama unfolds just as the shepherds are going to their customary meeting place, the *fuente de alisos,* in the heat of the day. This reference is pertinent, for it reinforces the point made earlier concerning the traditional association of the hot hours of the day with the actions of the devil, a view shared by the Psalmist who, in one breath, pleads for deliverance from "hostile attacks" and from the "noon-day demon" (Psalm 90.3-6). Understandably Milton has Satan tempt Eve at midday: "Meanwhile the hour of noon drew on, and waked / An eager appetite, . . . / So saying her rash hand in evil hour / Forth reaching to the fruit, she plucked, she eat" (*Paradise Lost,* 9.739-40, 780-81).

Felismena's agile, courageous, and almost knightly conduct seems to fulfill Montemayor's call to an active life in the service of God, proclaimed in his *Diálogo spiritual,* where he invites man to "entrar en la orden de cavallería del Señor y lidiar con el demonio."[20] Since the Middle Ages the slaying of the wild man had been symbolic of "the removal of a personified obstacle to the return of spring, a winter demon who had to be killed so that his icy breath would not impede the sprouting of greenery."[21] In fact, as Richard Bernheimer has noted, the oldest *ludus de homine salvatico* was a spring festival held at the time of Pentecost, while other wild-man rituals were held at Carnival time, thus at a period of the year interpreted as terminating the winter as well as opening the door for the new season.[22] Theological expression of the wild man's wickedness is to be found in the book of sermons written by the fifteenth-century German writer Geiler of Kaysersberg, entitled *Die Emeis* (The Ant); there the wild man is referred to as the "devil's ghost" intent on intruding on Christian society.[23]

As A.D. Deyermond pointedly notes, in the wild men of folklore are concentrated and personified those aspects of humanity that are dangerous to society and religion, and as such are to be

20. Cited by Mario Martins, "Uma obra inédita de Montemôr," 406.
21. Richard Bernheimer, *Wild Men in the Middle Ages* (Cambridge, Mass., 1952), 56.
22. Ibid.
23. Ibid., 60.

excluded from the civilized world.[24] The bucolic reaction to might and violence is "primarily sentimental," says Renato Poggioli; "the consciousness of its own innocence, merging with the awareness that the precariousness of its happiness is due to acts of men rather than to 'acts of God,' produces in the pastoral soul a sense of outraged justice."[25] The gruesome fate met by the wild men at the hands of Felismena, who kills two of them by piercing their hearts with her arrows and the third by launching an arrow through his eye, is seen as just punishment for their evil deeds: "¿No merecían menos pena que la que tienen?" Felismena asks the nymphs (91). The savages are duly punished for their "mal conocimiento" but also for their "orgullo" (91), a sin toward which Montemayor shows particular contempt.[26] Thus, rather than being merely an example of esthetic contrast, as some have suggested,[27] the episode of the wild men attacking the nymphs serves to elucidate the disruptive effect of unchaste or sensual love, the antithesis of honest or spiritual love, that goal so nobly espoused by the Neoplatonic lover.

The contrast between sensual and spiritual love is dramatized further by the setting whence the savages come. Whereas the waters of the *locus amoenus* are invariably described as "calm," "pure," and "crystalline," the river crossing the "escura y encantada" forest in which the wild men dwell is "impetuoso y turbio" (88), a vivid symbol of the savages' violence and sinfulness, as are the "temerosos campos" (88) irrigated by their river. In addition, we will recall that the nymphs are attacked by the wild men in the field of laurels (89), plants sacred to Apollo, the goddess Diana's twin brother. In mythology the Maenads, orgiastic priestesses of Daphne, the mountain nymph, chewed laurel leaves as an intoxicant and, periodically rushing out of the woods at the full moon, assaulted unwary travelers and tore children or young animals to pieces; laurel contains cyanide of potassium.[28]

24. Alan D. Deyermond, "El hombre salvaje en la novela sentimental," *Actas del Segundo Congreso Internacional de Hispanistas* (Nijmegen, 1967), 265.

25. *Oaten Flute,* 183.

26. See López Estrada, "La epístola de Jorge de Montemayor," 380-85.

27. See, for example, Wardropper, "The *Diana* of Montemayor," 141.

28. Robert Graves, *The Greek Myths* (Baltimore, 1955), 1: 167, 18.

By killing the lustful wild men, Felismena symbolically teaches the shepherds and shepherdesses to distinguish between virtue and vice, imparting to them prudence, a key virtue of the Christian pilgrimage. Felismena, we will recall, casts away her city clothing and takes on the robes of a "pastora" in what could well be inter preted as a symbolic transformation of the courtly lady into a priestess, keeping in mind the traditional conjunction of meanings in the word "pastor" as both shepherd and priest.[29] In all respects Felismena is represented as the fulfillment of justice and the spirit of consolation, very much as the Virgin is depicted in one of Montemayor's couplets to Our Lady.[30]

The unique place occupied by Felismena among the wayfaring shepherds and shepherdesses is later dramatized by the fact that it is she who reads the moral warnings inscribed on the entrance to the palace and who calls them "leyes" (166). Her singular role is symbolically seen by yet another event. After receiving Felicia's gratitude for having saved her nymphs from the wild men, only she is given a place in Felicia's own quarters so that they may converse alone (171). While Selvagia and Belisa keep their rustic clothing, Felismena is singled out by being elegantly dressed by the nymphs, who adorn her with spiritually and allegorically symbolic jewels.

Following his practice of extracting a symbolic meaning from material objects in order to point a moral lesson, as seen in his early work *Exposición moral sobre el salmo LXXXVI*,[31] Montemayor uses the jewels as carefully executed vehicles of didacticism. The intelligent examination of these precious stones made by Francisco Márquez Villanueva discloses a wide range of symbolic and allegori cal connotations which enrich and strengthen the instructive nature of *Diana*, while confirming the exalted role of Felismena in the novel. Crystal, with which the stems of Felismena's earrings are made, had been considered since the early Middle Ages as a symbol of the spirit. The transparent quartz plausibly represents in *Diana* the purity of the soul in the state of grace, a condition sym-

29. Cf. Marinelli, *Pastoral*, 10.

30. *Obras* (Antwerp, 1554), 133–34. See Creel, "Religious Poetry," 293–94.

31. Cf. López Estrada, "La exposición," 503.

bolized by a perfect diamond for St. Teresa of Ávila.[32] Parenthetically, it is well to point out that Felismena's forehead is characterized as "cristalina" (172), a further symbol of her freedom from
fault or guilt, in contrast to Diana, who is guilty of inconstancy.
The naviform earrings worn by Felismena are also highly connota-
tive. A rare example of a gold enamelled pendant in the shape of a
boat, probably of Venetian work, and similar to the one described
by Montemayor, is in the Victoria and Albert Museum of London.
The ship "typified the Holy Church of Christ,"[33] possibly symbolized in *Diana* by the collective body of shepherds and shepherdesses moving toward Felicia's palace under the protection of
Felismena. Since Horace (*Odes* 3.1), the ship had also been treated
in conjunction with hope, and the "ship of hope" was a frequent
image in secular, spiritual, and emblematic literature of the Renaissance.[34] Felismena, who heroically pursues her goal of finding her
loved one, never wavering in her mission, can truly be said to
exemplify the virtue of hope. Not surprisingly, Felicia rewards the
relentless Felismena with the renewed and reassuring hope of ful-
filling her "virtuoso fin" (171) of finding Felix. Felismena's hopeful
nature is symbolized by the splendid emeralds from which the earrings are carved, whose green color is itself a symbol of hope.[35] Not
only does the emerald stand for hope, recommended for passions of
the heart, but also it is suggestive of the resplendent just soul,[36]
a quality that eminently characterizes Felismena, who justly protects
the nymphs and Felix from adversity.

The expressive function of Felismena's jewels is extended to the

---

32. Márquez Villanueva, "Los joyeles de Felismena," *Revue de littérature comparée* 52 (1978): 269–77. Márquez Villanueva (269) cites a most
useful bibliography to substantiate the symbolism of crystal, including the
very informative study by Gaspar de Morales, *Libro de las virtudes y pro-
piedades maravillosas de las piedras preciosas* (Madrid, 1605), 201 v.

33. Bayley, *New Light,* 255.

34. The point is well presented and amply documented by Márquez
Villanueva ("Los joyeles," 270), who recalls the use made of the symbolic
barquillas by Lope de Vega in his *La Dorotea*; cf. Edwin S. Morby, "A foot-
note on Lope de Vega's Barquillas," *Romance Philology* 6 (1953): 289–93.

35. These observations are made by Márquez Villanueva, "Los joyeles,"
271.

36. Gaspar de Morales, *Libros de las virtudes,* 40 v, 101 v, 103 v, cited by
Márquez Villanueva, "Los joyeles," 272 nn. 25, 26.

three oriental pearls that garnish her headwear. In the oriental tradition the pearl awakens love in the one who bears it, while Christian
writings beginning with St. Isidore declare this gem to be a sign of
innocence and humility.[37] The union of the beautiful with the good
as a conception of art was first suggested by Socrates, who regarded
the beautiful as coincident with the good, and both of them as
resolvable into the useful. Accordingly, the philosopher minimized
the importance of the immediate gratification which a beautiful
object affords to perception and contemplation, and stressed instead
its power in furthering the more necessary ends of life.[38] To those
ends, the sapphires enchased in the jewelry that decorates the scarlet
band with which Felismena is symbolically crowned are also significant. The sapphire, formed of transparent rich blue corundum, has
been associated with the firmament and has thus come to signify
morally the values of steadfastness and immutability,[39] qualities
highly representatative of Felismena.

The emerging visual portrait of Felismena is part of the novelist's
effort to eternalize, as it were, Felismena and her virtues in a specific
moment of her life. This becomes particularly significant if we bear
in mind that until the Baroque era the general norm was to make
portraits only of nobility and others of high social rank,[40] as Felismena certainly is. Anticipating a technique frequently found in
Baroque portraits, Montemayor depicts Felismena in a fantastic
setting, adorned with a generous complement of objects which have
a symbolic and allegorical function in relation to her character. One
of the most intriguing objects adorning Felismena is a "collar de
oro fino, hecho a manera de culebra enroscada que de la boca
tenía colgada una águila que entre las uñas tenía un rubí grande de
infinito precio" (172). The serpent in the form of a circle, "culebra
enroscada," frequently portrayed in Renaissance emblematic tradi-

37. Márquez Villanueva, "Los joyeles," 271; he cites the symbolic value of
the pearl as used by, among others, Raban Mauro and Dante, the latter com-
paring it to the active souls of Paradise.

38. Cf. John W. Beatty, *The Relation of Art to Nature* (New York, 1922),
16.

39. The sapphire has also been found to be a "conspicuous symbol of
hope"; see Márquez Villanueva ("Los joyeles," 273), who cites examples from
a French medieval poet and from Dante (*Purgatorio*, 1.13).

40. Emilio Orozco Díaz, *Amor, poesía y pintura en Carrillo do Sotomayor*
(Granada, 1967), 37.

tion, symbolized universality or omnipresence, and (because it offers no solution of continuity) likewise of eternity.[41] The coiled snake is also representative of the inscrutability of the Divine Being,[42] a popular idea in eastern architecture and among the Guild of Cathedral Builders known as the Comacine Masters. At times the coiled snake was further represented in emblematic literature as a symbol of prudence, as well.[43] The symbol is worthy of Felismena, whose love is unbending and who governs and disciplines herself by the use of reason. Equally appropriate to her character is the symbol of valor and generosity associated with the eagle hanging from the serpent's mouth.[44] As for the ruby encased between the claws of the eagle, it should be noted that it not only was considered the supreme gem in the Renaissance, but was also an object of almost sacred prestige, and as such became a stupendous allegorical tool for the representation of the perfect enamoured heart.[45] Thus it is a most fitting tribute to Felismena. That the vivid description of the headdress and neckware should begin and end with a ruby is indeed indicative, as Márquez Villanueva has noted, of the special significance attributed to this gem by Montemayor, who professes throughout *Diana* that beauty is of spiritual, not physical, origin.[46] The description of Felismena's necklace evokes the image of those emblems so popular in Renaissance and Baroque Europe whose history has been perceptively traced by Mario Praz and Karl Ludwig Selig,[47] among others. Although, as Márquez Villanueva has noted,

41. Bayley, *New Light*, 25.
42. Ibid.
43. See Arthur Henkel and Albrecht Schöne, *Emblemata* (Stuttgart, 1967), cols. 652-59; and G. de Tervarent, *Les énigmes de l'art: L'héritage antique* (Paris, 1946), cols. 340-42. Both works are cited by Márquez Villanueva, "Los joyeles," 275 n. 40.
44. E. Ingersoll, *Birds in Legend, Tale and Folklore* (New York, 1923), 150, cited by Márquez Villanueva, "Los joyeles," 274 n. 41.
45. Márquez Villanueva, "Los joyeles," 275, 276.
46. This view is expressed by Márquez Villanueva ("Los joyeles," 276), who echoes the observations made by Bruce Wardropper, "The *Diana* of Montemayor," 41; and Antonio A. Cirurgião, "O papel da beleza na *Diana* de Jorge de Montemor," *Hispania* 51 (1968): 402-7.
47. Mario Praz, *Studies in Seventeenth Century Imagery* (Rome, 1964); Karl Ludwig Selig, "The Spanish Translation of Alciato's *Emblemata*," *Modern Language Notes* 70 (1955): 354-59.

no such precious object has been preserved from the sixteenth century, it does appear in a celebrated portrait of Simonetta Vespucci by Piero di Cosimo.[48] The portrait, found in the Musée Condé de Chantilly, is said to represent Simonetta as Proserpina,[49] daughter of Ceres, goddess of grain and harvest. Parenthetically it is worth noting that a character named Proserpina, a pleading figure, appears in the song of Orpheus in Poliziano's pastoral opera *Orfeo* (verses 286–301), written in 1480. In *Diana*, Orpheus will dedicate his song first to Felismena and then to the other guests at Felicia's palace.

A representation of a figure similar to that found on Felismena's necklace appears also in two emblems of Joachim Camerarius and George Wither, both subsequent to the publication of *Diana*.[50] Discussing the influence of Wither's emblems on the work of Crashaw, the critic Marc F. Bertonasco affirms: "George Wither provides us with an interesting example of a reproduction of one of Camerarius' plates: an eaglet is perched on a winged ball, which in turns rests on an altar. On each side serpents unsuccessfully attack the bird. Virtue aspires to sublime heights and is indifferent both to earthly blessings, which it sees as ephemeral and fickle, and to the attacks of worldlings."[51] The eagle, then, represents, as Frederick A. de Armas has noted, the "flight toward perfection and virtue,"[52] qualities eminently displayed by Felismena.

The allegorical moralizing in Montemayor's highly symbolic treatment of Felismena's jewelry is not surprising in a man purported to have written a book on blazons,[53] an enigmatic art form that comprises heraldic and armorial bearings. The scrupulous attention to detail that characterizes the description of Felismena's attire and jewels relates well to:

48. "Los joyeles," 273.
49. See M. Bacci, *Piero di Cosimo* (Milan, 1966), 67–68.
50. I am indebted for this information to my good friend Frederick A. de Armas, "Las tres Dianas," 190.
51. Marc F. Bertonasco, *Crashaw and the Baroque* (University, Ala., 1971), 31, cited by de Armas, "Las tres Dianas," 190.
52. "Las tres Dianas," 90.
53. Jorge de Montemayor, *Libro de blasones,* cited by Domingo García Perés, *Catálogo razonado biográfico y bibliográfico de los autores portugueses que escribieron en castellano* (Madrid, 1890), 391.

the immense care and learning which was spent on the "correct" equipment of figures not only in paintings but also in masques and pageantries where nobody but the organizers themselves could ever hope to understand all the learned allusions lavished on the costumes of figures which would only appear for a fleeting moment. Perhaps the idea was under the threshold of consciousness that by being in the "right" attire these figures became genuine "masks" in the primitive sense, which turn their bearers into the supernatural beings they represent. Justice welcoming the King at the city gate during a "Glorious Entry" was perhaps conceived as more than just a pretty girl wearing a strange costume. In and through her, Justice herself had come down to earth to greet the ruler and to act as a spell and an augury.[54]

Writing about the Latin pastoral, Bruno Snell observes that the heritage of the Greeks is turned, in Virgil's *Eclogues,* into "allegory and literature is transformed into a kingdom of symbols."[55] That strain of allegory and symbolism is amplified in *Diana* as the shepherds continue their pilgrimage to the palace of the wise Felicia.

On the way to the palace the shepherds and shepherdesses pass through a "thick forest" by a path so narrow "por donde no podían yr dos personas juntas" (163), a vivid reminder of Holy Scripture's description of the road to heaven: "Because strait is the gate, and narrow is the way, which leads unto life, and few there be that find it" (Matt. 7.14). Among those who find the path of salvation are those "who have borne the burden of the day and the scorching heat" (Matt. 20.12), a further reminder of the characters of *Diana,* who have endured the toil of their passion in the hours of most intense heat. As the wayfarers approach the palace they are greeted by several nymphs, all dressed in "telillas blancas" (163), as are the elders in the Book of Revelation (4.4). Their "dorados cabellos" are crowned with "guirnaldas de flores," another possible allusion to the angelic beings of the heavenly court who bear "golden crowns

54. E.H. Gombrich, *"Icones Symbolicae*: The Visual Image in Platonic Thought," *Journal of the Warburg and Courtauld Institutes* 11 (1948): 178.
55. Bruno Snell, "Arcadia: The Discovery of a Spiritual Landscape," in *The Discovery of the Mind,* trans. T.G. Rosenmeyer (New York, 1968), 306.

upon their heads" (Rev. 4.4). These and other parallels with scriptural writings suggest that, although perhaps not a son of the
classical tradition, Montemayor was unquestionably the "filho da
Sagrada Escritura," in the words of Mario Martins, who refers to
him as "um dos escritores mais sensíves à beleza dos Livros
Santos."[56] In the "Prólogo al lector" of the *Diálogo spiritual,*
Montemayor himself discloses his positive regard for the Bible since
the days of his infancy.[57] His fervent religious inclinations, based to
a large degree on scriptural readings, ensured him the reputation of
having dramatized the esthetic and moral values of the Bible in a
century curious about things classical.

Behind the nymphs there comes Felicia, "una dueña que, según
la gravedad y arte de su persona, parecía muger de grandissimo
respecto, vestida de raso negro, arrimada a una nimpha muy más
hermosa que todas" (163). As a sign of that respect, first the
nymphs and then the shepherds and shepherdesses kiss her hand
"con grandíssima humildad" (163). Since it may be presumed that
the hand kissed is the right hand, it is well to point out that the right
hand has in all ages been deemed an important symbol of the virtue
of fidelity. "Among the ancients the right hand and fidelity to an
obligation were almost indeed synonymous terms."[58] Significantly,
however, as Felismena bows herself to pay homage to Felicia in a
similar manner, the sage lady embraces her lovingly (165), thereby
stressing the singular position that Felismena holds among the characters of the novel. The simple but highly symbolic gesture of the
embrace is relevant to a definition once given by William Empson
to the pastoral as essentially the "process of putting the complex
into the simple."[59]

Following her embrace of Felismena, the wise Felicia reveals her
omniscience to her special guest. She informs the noble woman
turned shepherdess of her knowledge of Felismena's background and
amorous conflict, and of her victory over the wild men which saved
the nymphs' lives, for which she vows eternal help: "lo que por estas
tres nimphas avéis hecho, no se puede pagar con menos que con
tenerme obligada siempre ser en vuestro favor" (163), adding "ya

56. "Uma obra inédita," 400.
57. Cited in ibid., 401.
58. Bayley, *New Light,* 72.
59. William Empson, *Some Versions of Pastoral* (London, 1950), 23.

entenderéis si os puedo aprovechar en algo," thus hinting at her omnipotence, as well. Felicia's universal knowledge is reiterated at the end of the novel, where we are told that the wise lady knew of the shepherds' coming to her palace (299). Felicia acknowledges and praises Felismena for having endured her toils, telling her: "aunque ayáis passado algunos trabajos, no ay cosa que sin ellos alcançar se pueda" (163). (Montemayor's belief in the value of works has been noted.[60] His beliefs, in this respect, were consistently orthodox.[61])

The formality of greeting completed, the shepherds, shepherdesses, nymphs, and Felicia all together enter the "sumptuoso palacio" (164): "una gran casa de tan altos y sobervios edificios que ponían gran contentamiento a los que los miravan porque los chapiteles que por encima de los árboles sobrepujavan, davan de sí tan gran resplandor que parecían hechos de un finísimo crystal" (163) ". . . toda la casa parecía hecha de reluziente jaspe" (165). The rare luminescence reminds us of the splendor of allegorical visions of the afterlife found in several examples of medieval literature.[62] The philosophical and religious cult of light, "the most noble element of the integral culture of antiquity," goes back to Neoplatonic and stoic writers and to St. Augustine,[63] and Holy Scripture relates the holy city of Jerusalem to a "light [that] was like a stone most precious, even like a jasper stone, clear as crystal" (Rev. 21.11). Appropriately, in his suberb book on the visual image in Neoplatonic thought, E.H. Gombrich makes the point that "God has revealed the truth about the supernatural world in the strange images taken from the sensible world."[64]

As for the "tall and lofty buildings" that make up the palace, these too echo the description of the "wall great and high" of the Holy City (Rev. 21.12). The "casa quadrada" with a "muy alta y artificiosa torre," in front of which was a square "enlosada con losas

60. *El cancionero del poeta Jorge de Montemayor* (Madrid, 1932), 122, 244; also, Montemayor, *Segundo Cancionero* (Antwerp, 1558), 33r.

61. Bataillon, *Une Source de Gil Vicente*, 36–40.

62. See María Rosa Lida de Malkiel, "La visión del trasmundo en las literaturas hispánicas," appendix to Patch, *El otro mundo*, 408–22.

63. José María Sánchez de Muniain, *Estética del paisaje natural* (Madrid, 1945), 145.

64. Gombrich, "*Icones Symbolicae*," 167.

de alabastro y mármol negro, a manera de xedrez'' with a "fuente de mármol jaspeado" and a "columna de jaspe" facing a "portada de mármol" (165), shares further similarity with the scriptural reference to precious stones and marbles and the overall emphasis on detail that characterizes the description of Jerusalem, a city that "lies foursquare," with structures of jasper and other precious stones (Rev. 21.15-21).[65] These similarities invite me to note briefly a comment on the pastoral by Edward William Tayler, who points out that the novel about shepherds "has become a vehicle in a very strict sense, a form for the allegorical expression of a variety of different subjects. This use of pastoral was of immense importance for the Renaissance: there, behind the traditional locutions, lay the truths of Revelation, and the most conventional phrases reverberate with biblical overtones."[66]

Regarding Montemayor's meticulous description of Felicia's palace, it is well to enlist again the opinions of E.H. Gombrich concerning the artistic use of objects in the Renaissance:

> The objects in our sublunar world have different qualities. Some, like heat and cold, dryness and moisture, are elemental and thus wedded to the world of matter. Others, like brightness, colours and numbers—that is proportion—appertain both to our sublunar world and to the celestial sphere. These mathematical shapes and proportions, then, belong to the higher order of things. Shapes and proportions, therefore, have the most intimate connection with the Ideas in the World Soul or the Divine Intellect. *"Imo et cum idaeis maximam habent in mente mundi regina connexionem."* What applies to numbers and shapes applies also to colours, for colour is a kind of light which is itself the effect and image of the intellect.[67]

Having come to the door of the palace, the shepherds "se pararon a mirar su estraña hechura y las imágines que en ella avía, que más

65. I wish to express my gratitude to Frederick D. Phillips for calling to my attention the Book of Revelation and other parts of the Bible as possible sources of *Diana.*

66. *Nature and Art,* 97.

67. *"Icones Symbolicae,"* 177.

parecía obra de naturaleza que de arte ni aun de industria humana" (165). Considering the association of nature with providence,[68] it now becomes even more apparent that the shepherds are standing before a celestial paradise, a *terra repromissionis sanctorum,* a holy place of reward for the toils endured by the pilgrims. The idea of wayfarers in exile who find a place of rest from a troubled life in a well built and secure place had already been presented by Montemayor in his *Exposición moral sobre el salmo LXXXVI.* There the place of repose is a city built high on a mountain, allegorically the "city of God," personified by the Blessed Virgin.

In *Diana* not only is the palace a holy place, but Felicia herself betrays saintly qualities, as she reveals by her first words to the gathered wayfarers: "Animosos pastores y discretas pastoras; no tengáis miedo a la perseverancia de vuestros males pues yo tengo cuenta con el remedio dellos" (164). The cure begins with a "penitential" rite that demands of the shepherds and shepherdesses an examination of conscience as called for by a set of "laws" (166) inscribed on a tablet held up by two nymphs upon the main entrance to the palace. Echoing an admonition found in Holy Scripture that the unworthy shall not enter heaven (Rev. 21.27), the copper tablet engraved with gold letters bears the following words:

> Quien entra, mire bien cómo a bivido
> y el don de castidad, si le a guardado
> y la que quiere bien o lo a querido
> mire si a causa de otro se a mudado.
> Y si la fe primera no a perdido
> y aquel primer amor a conservado
> entrar puede en el templo de Diana
> cuya virtud y gracia es sobrehumana.
>   [165]

The allegorical entrance-way into the palace reminds us of the "porta velha" of peace and tranquillity mentioned in the *Diálogo spiritual,* that "last allegorical door of heaven" sustained by three

---

68. Otis H. Green, *Spain and the Western Tradition: The Castilian Mind in Literature from El Cid to Calderón* (Madison, Wis., 1968), 1: 89 n. 68.

symbolic arches of faith, hope, and charity that make happy he who enters it.[69] The octave inscribed at the entrance of Felicia's palace recreates the ancient theme of the "prueba de amor," "which was a common topic of the Byzantine novel and later appeared repeatedly in chivalresque literature."[70] The inscription is an important part of the novel's overall didacticism, achieved through what Ronald Carpenter would call a "functional style" designed to create "relevant and specific psychological effects on the part of readers or listeners."[71] As Cicero reminds us, the function of style is to influence hearers, to attract and hold their attention, to persuade, to move.[72]

With the inscription, and the already evidenced importance that the sage Felicia places on suffering to gain perfection—and salvation—, the shepherds are reminded of human guilt. The fact that the shepherdess Diana is the only character who cannot enter into the palace, referred to in the inscription as the "Temple of Diana," is indicative of the significance that Montemayor attached to inconstancy as a sin. Consequently there is instilled in the shepherds a spirit of self-examination and reproach reminiscent of the manner in which Montemayor reproves himself in some of his religious poetry, particularly the *Soliloquio* that begins the devotional works in the 1554 *Cancionero*.[73] In that poem, we will recall, Montemayor, using dialogue form, alternately addresses himself as "sinner" and admonishes himself.

After having taken heed of the warning carved on the portal, and only after this act of humility is fulfilled, the shepherds are admitted into the palace, but not before being reminded once again of the miraculous events about to take place there. "No te congoxes," Felicia assures Sireno, "que antes de muchos días te espantarás de averte congoxado tanto por essa causa" (166). Comforted by those

69. Pertinent textual passages from the *Diálogo spiritual* are cited by Martins, "Uma obra inédita," 407.

70. Avalle-Arce, "The *Diana* of Montemayor," 6.

71. Ronald D. Carpenter, "Stylistic Redundancy and Function in Discourse," *Language and Style* 3 (1970): 62.

72. *Orator*, trans. H.M. Hubbell, in *Readings in Classical Rhetoric*, ed. T.W. Benson and M.H. Prosser (Bloomington, Ind., 1972), 238.

73. Pp. 119–22.

words, the shepherds and shepherdesses walk into the palace and, in an ecumenical gesture of "holding hands," proceed directly to an opulent dining room:

> Y luego que fueron entradas, la cena se aparejó, las mesas fueron puestas, y cada uno por su orden, se assentaron; junto a la gran sabia, la pastora Felismena y las nimphas tomaron entre sí a los pastores y pastoras, cuya conversación les era en extremo agradable. Allí las ricas mesas eran de fino cedro y los asientos de marfil con paños de brocado; muchas taças y copas hechas de diversa forma y todas de grandíssimo precio; las unas, de vidrio artificiosamente labrado; otras, de fino crystal con los pies y asas de oro; otras, de plata y entre ellas engastadas piedras preciosas de grandíssimo valor. Fueron servidos de tanta diversidad y abundancia de manjares, que es impossible podello dezir. [166]

The ritualistic seating arrangements of her guests is also highly symbolic. Felismena, the most virtuous of the wayfarers for her constancy and hopefulness, is rewarded with a position of greatness in proximity to the hostess, the dispenser of hope, while the rustic pilgrims are seated alternately next to the nymphs, symbols of chastity, the very virtue exacted of those who enter the palace.

It has been noted that by the time of Horace "every poetic landscape has its altar."[74] In Montemayor's novel there is an altar in the Temple of Minerva to which shepherdesses bring their prayers and offerings (41–42), and there is also Felicia's highly symbolic dining table, which performs a function analogous to that of an altar. The mysterious nature of what is served may well symbolize the spriitual nourishment given by Felicia to her guests. The fact that nothing at all is said about what the shepherds eat is significant also for another reason. The senses of taste, smell, and touch are altogether missing from the Temple of Diana, since these senses were considered to be conducive only to *amor ferinus.*[75] Accordingly Montemayor opts for the noble and spiritually edifying visual experience of his charac-

74. Rosenmeyer, *Green Cabinet,* 127.
75. Panofsky, *Problems in Titian,* 120.

ters, in consonance with the Platonic position so forcefully defended by art theorists of the Renaissance. But since the eye perceives only the beauty of the body, as stressed by such contemporaries of Montemayor as the Venetian humanists Giuseppe Betussi and Pietro Bembo, and before them by Aristotle,[76] the author of *Diana* injects a good measure of acoustic experience to attain as well an understanding of the soul.

Thus, when supper is ended, the narrator continues, "entraron tres nimphas por una sala, una de las quales tañía un laúd, otra, una harpa y la otra, un psalterio. Venían todas tocando sus instrumentos con tan grande concierto y melodía, que los presentes estavan como fuera de sí" (166-67). The reference to the characters' ecstatic state can only have meaning in terms of what must surely be a "celestial" music played by the nymphs. The entire celebration in Felicia's palace is reminiscent of the wedding feasts witnessed by the mythical poet and singer Orpheus, as portrayed by medieval secular writers, who focused on such items as the dishes and glasses at the nuptial festivities, as well as the customs, the personal grace of the lovers,[77] and of course the ennobling music of Orpheus himself.

Following the musical interlude provided by the nymphs, who sing and play their instruments with the accompaniment of the shepherds and shepherdesses, Felismena is taken through several rooms into a pool where she bathes with the nymphs. The scene is significant both because it evokes the scriptural reference to heaven as a "house of many mansions" (John 14.2), and because the symbolic bathing suggests purification of the soul. After her symbolic immersion in a pool of "claríssima agua" (171), Felismena and the rustics are led into a large courtyard with richly ornate columns, mosaic walls, and several statues of outstanding men of antiquity, among them the "bravo Aníbal" and the "valeroso Scipión Africano . . . ejemplo de virtud y esfuerço" (173). There are also sculptures of famed Spanish heroes, including the Cid, "honra de España"; Fernán

76. Aristotle, *De sensu*, 1.437 A.3-17; *Metaphysics* A 1.980 A.24-980 B.25. For Giuseppe Betussi's dialogue, *Il Raverta* (Venice, 1544), see G. Zonta, *Trattati d'amore del Cinquecento* (Bari, 1912), 3 ff.; see also O. Brendel, "The Interpretation of the Holkham *Venus*," *Art Bulletin* 28 (1946): 65 ff.

77. Friedman, *Orpheus in the Middle Ages*, 162.

González, "honra y prez de la Española silla," a man of "gran
virtud" and "altos hechos"; Bernardo del Carpio, "honra y prez de
los Christianos," and Gonzalo Fernández de Córdoba, the most
famous general to serve under the Catholic kings (174-75).

The setting is carefully contrived to promote noble sentiments in
the impressed visitors to the sacred edifice of Lady Felicia. After
having marvelled at these models of virtue, the pilgrims are given yet
another aspiration to excellence as they are led first through the
palace's main hall and then into an inner court, both adorned with
sculptured figures and histories of illustrious women of Spain and of
other nations. Singled out for special comment are the celebrated
heroines of antiquity, Artemisia, Mausolus's wife, and Lucretia,
models of faithfulness, a reminder again of the virtue demanded of
those who enter Felicia's palace. In an apparent allusion to the
paradisiacal location of the shepherds, they are described as being
"En tan grande admiración . . . [de] las cosas que allí veyan, que no
sabian que dezir, porque la riqueza de la casa era tan grande; las
figuras que allí estavan, tan naturales; el artificio de la quadra, y
la orden que las damas allí retratadas tenían, que no les parecía
poderse imaginar en el mundo cosa más perfecta" (178).

Thus mesmerized by their new surroundings, the shepherds approach a silver fountain in the middle of the inner court next to
which sits Orpheus, whose music, in legend enchanted all the wild
beasts, trees, and rocks on Olympus and made cruel hearts grow mild
and humble.[78] Montemayor must have been intrigued by the figure
of Orpheus even before the writing of *Diana,* since in one of his
religious poems he pays tribute to the singer Francisco de Gracia by
calling him an "Orfeo christiano" (*Segundo Cancionero,* 1558,
203r-204v).[79] The introduction of Orpheus into the pages of *Diana*
evokes a variety of emotional situations associated with the myth of
Orpheus and Eurydice, including love, death, suspense, and rescue
from danger. Orpheus, like the shepherds and shepherdesses gathered
in Felicia's palace for whom he performs, was overcome by love and

78. Ibid., 88.
79. Cf. Michel Darbord, *La poésie religieuse espagnole des Rois Catho-
liques à Philippe II* (Paris, 1965), 421.

anxiety, but the use that Montemayor makes of him in *Diana* transcends this simple comparison. He is actually "resurrected" to inspire the shepherds to do good deeds, and in thus moving them away from their spiritual demise he serves out, symbolically at least, his traditional characterization as a psychopomp,[80] a guide of the souls after death.

As the legendary singer is approached by the nymphs, he takes up his harp and, turning to Felismena, begins to sing. Significantly, Orpheus avoids the use of a wind instrument, traditionally seen as appealing to the baser parts of the soul (St. Clement, *Paedogogus,* 2.iv), and plays instead the harp, the "noble" instrument by which David, God's helper, gave aid and comfort to Saul, thereby softening his evil spirit. To be noted, particularly, in terms of *Diana*'s pilgrimage is that the lyre and its offshoot the harp connected Orpheus with a body of Neoplatonic ideas about the harmony of the universe and the return of the soul to its celestial home.[81] We remember, too, that in mythology Orpheus played an important part in the expedition of the Argonauts (the band of heroes sailing with Jason in quest of the Golden Fleece), and that with his lyre he enabled them to resist the lure of the Sirens. The author of *Diana* is surely aware of this myth as he introduces Orpheus's music and song to help the group of wayfaring shepherds check their temptations.

The miraculous effect ascribed to music by the ancient Greeks, "the legends of Amphion and Orpheus, the stories of Pythagoras, Plato's beliefs in the . . . ennobling powers of music, all were constantly in the minds of the Renaissance musicians."[82] The effects of song and music on the spirit of man were emphasized in the Renaissance under the influence of the Neoplatonism of Marsilio Ficino, and by such respected musicologists as Anríquez de Valderrábano in the prologue to his *Silva de sirenas* (Valladolid, 1547) and Juan Bermudo in his *Declaración de instrumentos* (Osuna, 1549-55). As Castiglione reminds us, music has the power to "induce a good new

80. Friedman, *Orpheus in the Middle Ages,* 38–85, especially, 79.
81. Ibid., 82, 76.
82. Edward E. Lowinsky, "Music in Renaissance Culture," in *Renaissance Essays,* ed. Paul Oskar Kristeller and Philip R. Wiener (New York, 1968), 350.

habit of mind and an inclination to virtue, rendering the soul more capable of happiness, just as corporal exercise makes the body more robust."[83] The best synthesis of sixteenth-century Neoplatonists' views on music as it relates to the spiritual well-being of man is given by a leading authority of the time, Anríquez de Valderrábano:

Socrates (que fue tenido entre los philosóphos de su tiempo como verdadero oráculo) dezía que quando se iuntauan en el ánimo todos los desseos, affectos y movimientos della, y obedecían a la razón, se hazía de todo, como de bozes acordes, una armonía tan excelente y suaue, que despertaua al hombre y le hazía venir en consideración del mouimiento y consonancia de los cielos; y a ésta llamaua él verdadera música, y no sin causa, ca el entendimiento del hombre música es de gran perfectión, que con él se acuerdan las potentias sensitivas e intellectiuas, de do nace la consonancia de la razón, del conoscer, del sentir, del entender, y del juzgar lo bueno para huir lo malo. De que el diuino Platón dezía que la música principalmente fue dada para templar y moderar los affectos y passiones del alma. Fue tan estimada, que para encarecer la philosophía el mismo Platón y antes del los Pithagóricos la llamaron Música por serle semejante en los effectos. Esta música se causa y perfeciona de siete Sirenas que ay en el alma, que son siete virtudes, las quales despiertan el spíritu con su concordancia y armonía, para sentir y conoscer las cosas diuinas y humanas, y el gran bien que deste conoscimiento se sigue. Ésta en ninguna criatura terrena la puso Dios con tanta razón y perfectión como en el hombre, ni en los instrumentos de cuerdos como en el de la vihuela. Y assí es que lo que los sabios antiguos y todos los demás en loor de la música escriuieron parece claro que con mñas razón se deue atribuir a la vihuela, en que es la más perfecta consonancia de cuerdas.[84]

83. Baldesar Castiglione, *The Book of the Courtier*, trans. Charles S. Singleton (New York, 1959), 75.

84. Anríquez de Valderrábano, *Libro de música de vihuela intitulado "Silva de sirenas"* (Valladolid, 1547), 29.

In a symbolic gesture of selflessness, Orpheus expressly avoids singing "aquel processo largo de mis males" (180), and dedicates his octaves instead to exalting the beauty, goodness, wisdom, and purity of celebrated Spanish women. Following the tradition already established in fifteenth-century *Cancioneros* of singing praises to celebrated heroines of history and legend,[85] Montemayer lauds the noble qualities of forty-four women of the past and present while fusing in a uniquely characteristic manner historicolegendary material with national and patriotic motifs.[86] Luminous qualities, used earlier to characterize Felicia's palace, are now again employed with a didactic finality to describe the extraordinary beauty of the women praised by Orpheus. The women, all of whom represent moral virtues, are characterized in metaphorical terms that link them to celestial bodies:[87] "resplandor del sol," "luz que al orbe inflama," "sol que alumbra el mundo," "estrella que ciega" (180-90). In this the celebrated women serve symbolically as beacons to illuminate the path of life of these shepherds and shepherdesses, who are repeatedly called upon to focus their attention (with such words as "mirad," "veréis," "veis," "alçad los ojos") on the virtuous splendor of exemplary women. Lady Catalina Milán, one of the women eulogized by Orpheus for her superlative virtue, is referred to as a phoenix (186), a bird regarded in patristic literature as a symbol of the resurrection and of man's subsequent heavenly dwelling.[88]

Orpheus's song, true to legend, has such a mesmerizing effect on the pilgrim shepherds "de manera que los que le oyan, estavan tan agenos de sí que a nadie se le acordava de cosa que por él uviesse passado" (179), and the author later emphasizes that "assí los tenía suspensos, como si por ninguno dellos uviera passado mas de lo que presente tenían" (191). In Spanish music of the sixteenth century with texts in the vernacular, writes Don Randel, "nothing is reserved as belonging strictly in the province of only the secular or only the

85. Cf. Pierre Le Gentil, *La poésie lyrique espagnole et portugaise à la fin du Moyen Age* (Rennes, 1949), 1: 108.

86. Correa, "El templo de Diana," 69 n. 10.

87. Ibid., 70.

88. Gerhart B. Ladner, "Vegetation Symbolism and the Concept of Renaissance," in *De Artibus Opuscula XL: Essays in Honor of Erwin Panofsky,* ed. Millard Meiss (Zurich, 1960), 1: 318-19.

sacred,"[89] an observation that further strengthens the spiritually edifying component of Orpheus's music.

The position of the Song of Orpheus between the narratives of the shepherds' infirmity of passion and the cure of that passion by Felicia is also significant in terms of the traditional association of the myth of Orpheus with the theme of curiosity.[90] In the legend, so intense is the devotion Orpheus has for Eurydice that even against the precepts of the gods he is moved to look at his loved one, after which she is lost to him. It could well be that Orpheus's desire to see may be recalled in *Diana,* as his presence evokes a desire on the part of the shepherds and shepherdesses to attain greater insight into the mysteries of Felicia's palace.

To Neoplatonists "the myths were not only a mine of edifying metaphors. They were in fact yet another form of revelation. In accepting this belief the Neo-Platonists had no intention of minimizing the value of the Bible as the chief instrument of Divine revelation. On the contrary, they were convinced that the pagan lore rightly understood could only point towards the same truth which God had made manifest through the Scripture."[91] That pagan traditions were often not incompatible with Christianity is seen in Petrarch's reaction to Cicero's *De natura deorum,* in which the Italian humanist believed he had heard not the voice of a pagan philosopher but that of an apostle.[92] Similarly, Pico della Mirandola's *Teologia Platonica,* a work dealing with classical material, is also profoundly Christian. The great enthusiasm shown by Ficino and other Neoplatonists of his school for Horapollo Niliacus's *Hieroglyphica,* a work that claims to decipher the sacred symbols used in ancient Egypt, is another example of the way great minds of the Renaissance thrived on searching for spiritual meanings in mythical episodes of antiquity. Looking at the entire universe as a great myth endowed with spiritual meaning, Neoplatonists of Roman

89. Don M. Randel, "Sixteenth-Century Spanish Polyphony and the Poetry of Garcilaso," *Musical Quarterly* 60 (1974): 77.

90. Pablo Cabañas, *El mito de Orfeo en la literatura española* (Madrid, 1948), 63–74.

91. Gombrich, *"Icones Symbolicae,"* 169.

92. Marcel Bataillon, *Erasmo y España: Estudios sobre la historia espiritual del siglo XVI,* trans Antonio Alatorre (Mexico, 1966), 51.

antiquity and of the Renaissance defended those mythological legends which Cicero and Seneca scorned as "absurdities" and gave them pious and philosophical explanations.[93]

This task was particularly easy in treating Orpheus, who was after all not only considered the first singer of antiquity and an extraordinary poet, but also seen as the "principal theologian of Greece who instituted the mysteries to pacify the gods and save men."[94] He was thought to have established the Orphic sect, and his disciples composed books to propagate his ideas, his theogony, purifying formulas, and sacred hymns, all of which were attributed by his followers to Orpheus himself. The consideration of Orpheus as theologian persisted well into the seventeenth century in Spain with Fray Baltasar de Vitoria's *Primera parte del teatro de los dioses de la gentilidad.*[95]

It was in the sixteenth century, however, that the Christianization of Orpheus was vigorously promoted; he was depicted as "God's minister on earth" and was compared to the saints, specifically to St. John the Baptist.[96] St. John, we remember, preached repentance, "for the kingdom of heaven is at hand" (Matt. 3.2), and for this he was called upon to "prepare the way of the Lord, make his path straight" (Matt. 3.3). It is in this context that Orpheus, in Montemayor's novel, attains his highest significance, by serving as an inspirational force to the weary pilgrims and as the messenger and "angel" of Felicia who paves the way for the imminent and miraculous intervention.

After listening to Orpheus's laudatory song of exemplary Spanish women, the wayfarers move into the palace garden, which symbolizes yet another call to virtue. The lavish garden, whose sight causes "no menos admiración les causó que lo que hasta allí [los pastores] avían visto" (191), houses the graves of nymphs and ladies "las quales avían, con gran limpieza, conservado la castidad

93. Jean Seznec, *The Survival of the Pagan Gods* (New York, 1953), 100, 85.
94. Cabañas, *El mito de Orfeo*, 15.
95. Ibid., 15, 16.
96. Ibid., 153–57.

devida a la castíssima Diosa [Diana]" (191). For their steadfastness, these women have acquired glory and are immortalized in an allegorical conception of what is, after all, a temple of fame, itself a model to its wayfaring visitors.[97] As I noted in chapter 1, in the middle of the garden stands the tomb of Lady Catalina of Aragon y Sarmiento, a woman praised in history and literature for her outstanding faith and goodness. The adorning candlesticks with burning tapers symbolize these virtues. "It behoveth man," says a twelfth-century writer, "to have a candlestick that he may shine with good works," and there is a 1488 inscription on a candlestick which "by its good example inflameth others."[98] A century later Shakespeare exclaims "How far that little candle throws his beams! So shines a good deed in a naughty world."[99] Lady Catalina's tomb provides the shepherds and shepherdesses with a model in their pilgrimage toward "grace."

The tomb also points up the fact that in its entirety Felicia's palace guards the highest virtues of true lovers (constancy and chastity), which are contrasted to the condition of change and lascivious love exemplified by the shepherdess Diana and the wild men respectively.[100] In defense of the virtue of the visual image, Ficino expressed the view that the right image engraved on the right stone may have a potent effect on health.[101] The efficacy of the combined image and stone touches spiritual health, as well, for the visual image is morally instructive: "knowledge through symbols is higher knowledge."[102] Indeed, the sculptured figures around the tomb of Lady Catalina touch the heart of the beautiful Felismena and all who stand looking at the tomb and its epitaph (cited in chapter 1).

The emblem or device not only instructs us but, as E.H.

97. Cf. Chandler R. Post, *Medieval Spanish Allegory* (Cambridge, Mass., 1915); and Gustavo Correa, "El concepto de la fama en el teatro de Cervantes," *Hispanic Review* 27 (1959): 280–86, 299–302.

98. Bayley, *New Light,* 20, 21.

99. *The Merchant of Venice,* 5.1.90.

100. Correa, "El templo de Diana," 64.

101. Marsilio Ficino, *De vita coelitus comparanda* in *Opera Omnia* (Basle, 1576), 531 f., cited by Gombrich, "*Icones Symbolicae,*" 176.

102. Gombrich, "*Icones Symbolicae,*" 174.

Gombrich points out, "affects us." Arguments may convince, he goes on to say, but "images have a more direct impact on our mind. He who *sees* the truth can no longer err. He who is granted a vision of the supra-natural ideas becomes attuned to them."[103] Indeed, through inscriptions and the representations of tombs of nymphs and noble ladies, *Diana* presents the underlying thought that "man in his fallen state is a prey to death, but man redeemed inherits eternal life." The inevitability of death, suggested in *Diana,* is not a Christian theme "unless it is completed by some reference to the resurrection or the redemption of man."[104] Montemayor's novel fulfills this requirement by "resurrecting" its characters from their *desengaño,* from their misdirected passions to a new rational life through the allegorically sacramental intervention of Lady Felicia.

In the contemplation of tombs—mirrors of their own death—the characters of *Diana* discover the secret of their individuality.[105] They evolve from a seeming uniformity into distinct entities.

Before they journey to Felicia's palace the lovers are skeptical about the possibility of any remedy for their suffering. Sireno is convinced that every available option has already been exhausted (130), and Belisa doubts that even time will cure her ills (159). Like wayfarers in exile, estranged from God, the characters of *Diana* ultimately find a solution for their grief in the true home of love, the spiritual abode that is Felicia's palace. There lies the shepherds' only remedy: the miraculous intervention of Lady Felicia and what can rightly be called her "sacramental" water. "Olvidado pastor," says Felicia to Sireno, "si en tus males uviera otro remedio sino éste, yo te lo buscara con toda la diligencia possible" (223). "Confiad en Dios," says the sage lady to Felismena, "que vuestro desseo avrá buen fin, porque si yo de otra manera lo entendiera, bien podéis creer que no me faltarán otros remedios para hazeros mudar el pensamiento como a algunas personas lo e hecho" (223).

---

103. Ibid.

104. James M. Clark, *The Dance of Death in the Middle Ages and the Renaissance* (Glasgow, 1950), 67.

105. Philippe Ariès, *Western Attitudes toward Death: From the Middle Ages to the Present,* trans. Patricia M. Ranum (Baltimore, 1974), 51.

Unwilling to sustain the artificial passion tormenting his characters, the author resorts to a symbolic action with which he transforms the literary enigma of amorous impossibility into human love fulfilled. It is true, as Gustavo Correa has observed, that the transformation is brought on by the actions of superhuman entities (nymphs, the wise Felicia, and the goddess Diana), but the solution to misguided passion comes only "al final de una via purificatoria en el ejercicio del amor humano, el cual se ha tornado en arduo camino de renunciamento y heroísmo."[106] The process of spiritual purification continues in Felicia's palace, seen as a "mirror of the noble soul,"[107] where virtue is repeatedly extolled. The sage lady, the mythical Orpheus, and the sacred cemetery of nymphs and noble ladies in Book IV inspire virtuous sentiments in the shepherds and shepherdesses and, by extension, grace them with a degree of wisdom, a prerequisite to salvation.

Redemption for the characters of *Diana* begins when Sireno, from a vessel of fine crystal with a golden base, is given a magic potion which entirely removes his affection for Diana. Another "cruet," similarly made, is divided between Sylvano and Selvagia, who have been grieving for Diana and Alanio, respectively. On drinking the potions, these individuals fall insensible to the ground. A few moments afterward, Felicia awakens Sireno by touching him upon the head with a book which she has taken out of her sleeve (225). She then similarly awakens Sylvano, who on getting to his feet cries out: "¡O Selvagia, quán gran locura a sido aver empleado en otra parte el pensamiento, después que mis ojos te vieron" (226). Without avail he tries to awaken Selvagia. Felicia directs him to an adjoining room, and then awakens Selvagia as she has the other two. Selvagia's first words are : "Señora, ¿qué es del mi Sylvano? ¿No estava él junto conmigo? ¡Ay, Dios! ¿quién me lo llevó de aquí? ¡Si bolverá!" (227). Three significant points are to be noted in this account: first, that the change is brought about by a draught of magic liquid which induces sleep; second, that the persons are awakened, not naturally, but by the touch of a book; third, that the

106. "El templo de Diana," 63.
107. Perry, "Ideal Love," 230.

altered affection is predetermined by Felicia, not dependent upon the first thing sighted by the person on awakening.[108]

No magical water is administered to Felismena or Belisa, since both are of notable familes and therefore "enlightened." Unlike the "unlearned" shepherds, who must undergo a magical transformation in order to advance to a level of intellectual perception, Felismena and Belisa, already equipped with a measure of True Reason, and having enjoyed reciprocated affections, are left to solve their own amorous problems.[109] To do this, Felicia exhorts Felismena to have faith in God (223).

The next occurrence of altered affection is that of Felix. After Dórida, Felicia's nymph, has resuscitated the wounded knight sufficiently for him to understand her purpose, she addresses him with these words: "Cavallero, si queréis cobrar la vida y dalla a quien tan mala, a causa vuestra, la a passado [e.g., Felismena], beved del agua deste vaso" (297). Felix drinks from the golden flask and soon "se sintió tan sano de las heridas que los cavalleros le avían hecho y de la que amor, a causa de la señora Celia, le avía dado que no sentía más la pena que cada una dellas le podían causar que si nunca las uviera tenido. Y de tal manera se bolvió a renovar el amor de Felismena que en ningún tiempo le pareció aver estado tan vivo como entonces" (297).

Felicia's redeeming action brings to mind Walter Davis's interpretation of the action of pastoral romances. According to him, "the standard action consists of these elements in this order: disintegration in the turbulent outer circle [the world of romance], education in the pastoral circle and rebirth at the sacred center."[110] Such division of pastoral action complements Dante's theological division of human history into the era *ante legem*, the era *sub lege*, and the era *sub gratia*,[111] which correspond symbolically and respectively in *Diana* to the state of the shepherds in their passion, in the realm

108. Cf. T.P. Harrison, Jr., "Shakespeare and Montemayor's Diana," *Texas University Studies in English* 6 (1926): 98–99.

109. An observation made already by David H. Darst, "Renaissance Platonism and the Spanish Pastoral Novel," *Hispania* 52 (1969): 391.

110. Walter R. Davis, *A Map of Arcadia: Sidney's Romance and Its Tradition* (New Haven, 1965), 38.

111. Cf. Panofsky, *Studies in Iconology*, 55.

of the "leyes" of the Temple of Diana, and in the enjoyment of grace received from Felicia's draught.

Following the example set by Dante's mentor, Virgil, Renaissance writers looked for meaning in the pastoral, and the earliest formal criticism of the genre, Sebillet's "L'Art poétique françoys" (1548), emphatically calls for the use of allegory in pastoral literature.[112] Like Alexander Barclay before him, Philip Sidney would later argue that the allegorical content gives the pastoral the only value it has.[113] Allegory was a favorite tool of Renaissance man, who "was passionately interested in everything secret and esoteric and studied all available models wherever he could find them."[114] This propensity to use the mysterious and to hide deep meanings in it is certainly shared by Montemayor, whose *Diana* is pervaded by a subtle play of meaning and double meaning.

At first Felicia's magical intervention seems to be merely a part of the conventional and often entertaining action found in many romances that are built around a quest through which the hero acquires some secret knowledge or magic object which aids him in overcoming obstacles along the way. We will remember how Lancelot, in search of Guinevere, receives a magic ring to protect him from hostile enchantments, and how a knight in Marie de France's ballad *Les Deux Amanz* is given a vial of potion by an old, learned woman. The novelistic function of the magic draught in *Diana* has been the object of critical inquiry since the pronouncement made by the curate in *Don Quijote*'s famous scrutiny of the library: "Y pues comenzamos por la *Diana*, de Montemayor, soy de parecer que no se queme, sino que se le quite todo aquello que trata de la sabia Felicia y de la agua encantada" (*Quijote* 1.6). Américo Castro defends the attitude expressed by Cervantes, noting that what the great Spanish

112. See James Edward Congleton, *Theories of Pastoral Poetry in England, 1684-1798* (Gainesville, 1952), 26. This observation is also recorded by Evonne Buck in her fine doctoral dissertation, "Renaissance Pastoral Romance," 23.

113. Philip Sidney, "Defense of Poetry," cited by Congleton, *Theories of Pastoral Poetry*, 37–41; see also Buck, "Renaissance Pastoral Romance," 23.

114. Edward E. Lowinsky, *Secret Chromatic Art in the Netherlands Motet*, trans. Carl Buchman (New York, 1946), 135 n. 1, 153.

novelist condemns is the frivolity of Montemayor, for whom the erotic impulse, the most powerful vital essence, according to Cervantes, can change its nature and tone by means of a gulp of water.[115] Rather than "frivolity," the philter is a *deus ex machina* to Juan Bautista Avalle-Arce, who sees the water as easing plot developments hampered by the characters' inflexible attitude toward love (which stems from the Neoplatonic philosophy of the time).[116] It is in this context that T. Anthony Perry sees the wise Felicia as an "allegory" for the "desire and pursuit of happiness."[117] Significantly, as Gustavo Correa has noted, there is a certain psychological verisimilitude to the magic philter which turns grief into happiness. For Correa, the draught brings about a metamorphosis in the lovers through sleep which, with its healing action, comports an intensifying mechanism of time (forgetfulness) that shortens the period of waiting and presents solutions to insoluble problems.[118]

The magic philter, therefore, in addition to providing excitement and suspense as is so often the case in romances of chivalry, serves as a symbolic vehicle for the passage of time, which in turn brings about a change in the lovers' attitude toward love.[119] In this respect time serves as a "Revealer," known, as Erwin Panofsky points out, "not only from many proverbs and poetical phrases, but also from countless representations of subjects such as Truth revealed or rescued by Time, Virtue vindicated by Time, Innocence justified by Time, and the like."[120] Thus time, the destroyer of pastoral happiness, is also "the healer of wounds and producer of man's defense against sorrow, forgetfulness."[121] As the implications of the water of oblivion become clearer, so does the role of Felicia, whose portrayal finds a parallel of symbolic significance with the mythical god Anteros, who, according to a legend ignored in the Middle Ages but revived in the Renaissance, "was charged with the task of awakening

115. Américo Castro, *El pensamiento de Cervantes* (Barcelona, 1972), 150–51.
116. *La novela pastoril,* 55–82.
117. "Ideal Love," 233.
118. "El templo de Diana," 74.
119. On the "Water of Lethe" cf. Graves, *Greek Myths,* 1: 179.
120. *Studies in Iconology,* 83.
121. Jones, "Human Time," 145.

in those who were loved 'love in return' or avenging all kinds of offenses against the god of love."[122] Similarly, the representation of Felicia as promoter of well-being finds an analogue in a tenth-century drawing of Apollo Medicus and in a fifteenth-century drawing representing Apollo the Healer. The Felicia-Apollo parallel is particularly revealing in terms of *Diana*-as-pilgrimage, for it is Orpheus, Apollo's son, who through his symbolic call for virtue prepares the shelpherds for their redemption at the hands of Felicia.

The relationship of Felicia to Apollo is symbolically significant also if we bear in mind that Dante invokes Apollo at the beginning of his *Paradiso* (1.13). In the drawing of Apollo the Healer attributed to the Florentine painter Maso Finiguerra, Apollo is seen standing at a patient's bedside holding a book in his left hand and a partially filled flask in his right hand. Looking like an oriental magician in the act of resuscitating a dead person, the Apollo in Finiguerra's drawing has been associated with a "savior God, God of learned mysteries, God of life and of health-giving plants." In this respect the picture has gained the reputation of being "the most typical example of the tradition of the heroes and sages that places profane and sacred history on the same plane."[123] The identification of Christ with pagan figures was documented by an exciting discovery of one of the earliest Christian mosaics in the excavation of the Vatican cemetery under St. Peter's in the 1940s. Carefully examined by Marion Lawrence, this decoration depicts what he convincingly interprets to be the figure of Christ-Helios, "beardless as he appears in the catacombs, with girt tunic and flying mantle. . . . Behind His head are heavenly rays, which, stressing the vertical and the horizontals, suggest a great cross, but rayed like the sun and far larger than any Christian halo. He ascends to heaven triumphant in a chariot drawn by white horses. . . . all unlike the Ascension of Christ as we know it in early Christian art."[124]

Panofsky has stressed that the revival of classical motifs and classical themes is "only one aspect of the Renaissance movement in

122. Panofsky, *Problems in Titian*, 131.
123. Seznec, *Survival of the Pagan Gods*, 29, 28.
124. Marion Lawrence, "Three Pagan Themes in Christian Art," in *De Artibus Opuscula XL*, 333–34.

art."[125] Another equally important one is what he calls the "re-interpretation" of classical images, invested with new meaning and symbolism. Neoplatonic exegesis, which had presented such legendary figures as Apollo, Luna, and Ceres "with hitherto undreamed-of possibilities of reconciliation between the Bible and mythology, had now so obscured the distinction between the two that Christian dogma no longer seemed acceptable in anything but an allegorical sense."[126] Marsilio Ficino of Florence (1433-99), the most influential of the Neoplatonists, firmly believed that complete harmony existed between Platonism and Christianity. In fact, he devoted most of his life to the elucidation of Christian doctrine by means of Platonic concepts, which he placed on a par with the authority of those of the New Testament. In the words of Leonard Grant, "Ficino quite literally believed that Plato's work was divinely inspired."[127]

In view of the above, it is not too difficult to see the wise Felicia as a Christianized pagan god. Felicia's relationship to divinity intent on resurrecting the wayfaring shepherds from their spiritual death is strengthened by another parallel, this time with the figure of Christ himself holding in his hands a scroll, "no doubt the Book of Life," carved in the funeral chapel of the seventh-century French bishop, the Venerable Agilbert, in a portrayal of the Last Judgment.[128]

In a book by Philippe Ariès, *Western Attitudes toward Death*, we are reminded that, according to the general eschatology of the early centuries of Christendom, the dead who had entrusted their bodies to the care of the Church "went to sleep like the seven sleepers of Ephesus (*pausantes, in somno pacis*) and were at rest (*requiescant*) until the day of the Second Coming, of the great return, when they would awaken in the heavenly Jerusalem, in other words in Paradise." Similarly the dead who were not members of the Church

125. *Studies in Iconology,* 66 ff.

126. Seznec, *Survival of the Pagan Gods,* 99.

127. W. Leonard Grant, *Literature and the Pastoral* (Chapel Hill, N.C., 1965), 9.

128. J. Hubert, *Les cryptes de Jouarre* (IVe Congrès de l'art du haut moyen-âge) (Melun, 1952), cited in Ariès, *Western Attitudes toward Death,* 29. The tomb of the Venerable Agilbert, bishop of Dorchester and Paris, is found in the crypt of St. Paul's Church, Jouarre.

would not be awakened and would be abandoned "to a state of nonexistence."[129]

Ariès's comments suggest certain important parallels with *Diana*. In the novel the only pastoral figure unworthy of admission into Felicia's palace is the shepherdess Diana, because of her lack of fortitude and constancy. Accordingly, she is deprived of the miraculous healing bestowed upon her deserving sylvan friends, and subsequently becomes an outcast to the novel's pastoral society. By contrast, the other shepherds and shepherdesses share in the sleep of beatitude so intensely that in the words of Felismena, "Paréceme, señora, que si el descanso de estos pastores esta en dormir, ellos lo hazen de manera que vivirán los más descansados del mundo" (224), to which Felicia adds, "dormirán sin que baste *ninguna persona* a despertallos" (224, italics mine). The explicit reference to "ninguna persona" rather than the expected "nadie" dramatizes the exclusive role of Felicia as the sole entity capable of "resurrecting" the shepherds from their "sleep"—the sueño de la muerte" (227), as Sylvano describes it. When awakened by the sage lady Felicia with the book of knowledge, the revived shepherds will symbolically triumph over death and become truly the happiest characters of the pleasance.

The view stressed by Montemayor in his treatise *Carta de los trabajos de los reyes* that "la justicia no es cosa suya [del hombre], sino de Dios"[130] may lend support to the symbolic role of the wise Felicia as a godly figure. Seen thus, Felicia is not a mere agent who intercedes between man and the divine; she actually symbolizes the divine. In this context it is not "wizardry that saves man" but an allegorical action of God. The characters are not "drugged with a new sense of optimism based on a denial of the nature and implica-

---

129. P. 31.
130. In the text of this treatise reproduced by F.J. Sánchez Cantón, 50. On the question of justice in *Diana,* Rachel Bromberg offers the following observation: "Felicia's palace is a composite of the House of Fortune, the Palace of Love, the House of Fame, the court, a platonic academy, and a high-grade den of witchery. All these layers of meaning have been gathered into one area for one purpose—to bring about a union between nature and fortune, or worth and luck; in short, to enact justice" (*Three Pastoral Novels,* 61).

tions of their former agonies";[131] they are rather metamorphosed into new beings by divine grace. Parenthetically, it is interesting to note that it is characteristic of Montemayor's devotional poetry to "emphasize man's ultimate dependency on grace," as Bryant L. Creel has shown, and to represent "man as being helpless and abject without that grace."[132] As Montemayor exalts grace in his religious verses, so does Felicia extol the qualities of her miraculous water, which the distraught shepherds and shepherdesses drink with an attitude of reverence. The intervention of one of the nymphs, who restores Felix to reason by sprinkling him with a symbolic water of baptism, reinforces the exclusive power of grace.

Like a Eucharistic function, the redeeming action of Felicia is shrouded in mystery. Following his spiritual awakening Sireno simply acquiesces in the mystery:[133] "Yo estoy, discreta señora, satisfecho de lo que desseava entender y assí creo que lo estaré, según tu claro juyzio, de todo lo que quisiere saber de ti, aunque otro entendimiento era menester más abundante que el mío para alcançar lo mucho que tus palabras comprehenden" (198–99). The magic water, like grace, is an instrument of control and symbolizes victory over passion. The strength and efficacy of the water make the lovers insensitive to the external world, and in this the philter is analogous to the sacraments in bestowing the power to resist temptation. The philter, Felicia notes "sabe desatar los ñudos que este perverso del amor haze" (225). The symbolic significance of the liquid potion has been acutely perceived by T. Anthony Perry, for whom the philter "signifies a desire to purge and renew, water washes away, liquefies the hardened configurations of our destinies, restores the feeling of infinite possibility."[134] Thus at Felicia's palace, which Walter R. Davis would see as the novel's sacred center,[135] the characters undergo a process of rebirth. Spiritually regimented, they become like the pious faithful, instruments of divine will in the biblical message : "He restores my health: he leads me in the path of righteousness for his name's sake" (Psalm 23.3).

131. Oliveira e Silva, "*Arcadias* of Sir Philip Sidney," 14, 56.
132. "Religious Poetry of Montemayor," 97.
133. Perry, "Ideal Love," 228.
134. Ibid., 232.
135. "Masking in Arden," 38.

In restoring grace, with the miraculous philter and a book symbolic of her wisdom, Felicia also restores to the afflicted lovers the
power of reason. As Montemayor affirms, true love is born to
reason (195), but most lovers in *Diana* "se vienen a desamar a sí
mismos, que es contra razón y derecho de naturaleza" (196). With
the aid of the magic philter, the wise Felicia reestablishes the law of
nature and returns to the shepherds and shepherdesses "the power to
see reality and to evaluate it correctly."[136] Significantly, when
Sireno is awakened from his enchanted state, he arises "con todo su
juyzio" (225) and becomes what he really is, "Sireno, the serene
one."[137] The remedy for the soul lies in knowledge, and by imparting reason to the shepherds and shepherdesses, Felicia heals their
mental suffering and spiritual anguish.

Swayed by an intense emotionalism, the sixteenth century,
remarks Américo Castro, "buscará afanoso la virtud natural. . . . Pero
al mismo tiempo, el Renacimiento busca con no menor afán la
cultura, que es razón, y que es lo contrario de la espontaneidad
natural."[138] Indeed, reason was Renaissance man's "most cherished
possession, the faculty that separated him from the bestial hordes,
allied him with the angelic hosts, and permitted him to understand
an essentially rational universe."[139] That life according to reason is
best and pleasantest, as argued by Aristotle,[140] is illustrated by the
story of Felismena's mother, Delia, when she asserts that the inscription on the golden apple in the Judgment of Paris, "that it should be
given to the fairest," is to be understood as referring not to cor-
poreal beauty but to intellectual beauty (97). Felicia's argument that
true love springs from reason (195-97) lends further significance to
the supremacy of reason over any other human faculty.

True reason acquired through Felicia's philter moves the shepherds from a painful state of self-mortification to a new spirit of
real love and harmony, a renewed trust in human nature and a will

136. Jones, "Human Time," 146.
137. Perry, "Ideal Love," 232.
138. *El pensamiento de Cervantes,* 181.
139. Tayler, *Nature and Art,* 27.
140. *Nicomachean Ethics,* 10.7.1177b.30, trans. W.D. Ross, in Richard
McKeon, ed., *Basic Works of Aristotle* (New York, 1941).

to live,[141] and a fresh spirit of joy and confidence. Strengthened by the miraculous philter, Sireno can now even laugh at his past folly (225), with the author adding later that if it had not been for the potion, Sireno would still be helplessly discontented: "Si la fuerça del agua que la sabia Felicia le avía dado, no le uviera hecho olvidar los amores, quíçá no uviera cosa en el mundo que le estorvara bolver a ellos" (270). Cured of his former passion, Sireno can now look at Diana's flock, which once was witness to his suffering, and confidently sing out to the sheep: "Si venís por me turbar / no ay passión ni avrá turbarme / si venis por consolarme" (271). In the meantime, Diana, guilty of inconstancy, will remain forever disconsolate.

Like Sireno, the spiritually revived Sylvano can now look upon his former passion for Diana as madness: "¡O Selvagia, quán gran locura a sido aver empleado en otra parte el pensamiento, después que mis ojos te vieron!" (226). As a result of the potion Sylvano has left his unstable and restless life and has found a secure haven, a calm "puerto" where, he says, "plega a Dios que sea también recebido" (226), evoking with this the words of Scripture: "Surely goodness and mercy shall follow me all the days of my life: and I will dwell in the house of the Lord forever" (Psalm 23.6).

141. Cf. Darst, "Renaissance Platonism," 389; and Oliveira e Silva, "*Arcadias* of Sir Philip Sidney," 50.

Conclusion

The sociohistorical components of *Diana* are revealed in numerous ways: certain plausible traits of characterization, accurate and at times detailed rendering of an actual locality and temporal framework, autobiographical and other historical allusions, the use of Portuguese to achieve verisimilitude, an honest acknowledgment of human love and suffering, an examination of social problems and values (as well as fashions) of the time—all prove the dictum that "there is truth in concealment."[1] The love stories of persons in high life that *Diana* was known to conceal made it a riddle and a masquerade, engaging the curiosity of those who moved in Montemayor's circles. In his presentation of a whole "panorama of human experience,"[2] Montemayor anticipates the view expressed much later by Émile Zola that "all of nature and all of man belong to us."[3] A far cry this is from Estrella Gutierez's interpretation of *Diana* as a conventional novel that does not reflect any aspect of the real life of its years,[4] a novel in which the theme, setting, characters, and language are all "un mero artificio literario."[5] Quite the contrary, it may well be proper to see *Diana* as the pastoral world in general, "a microcosm of the greater world which magnifies as under a glass and for our better understanding, the very problems that press in upon us so confusingly there."[6]

It is precisely the presence of this social dimension that led Walter Greg to remark that *Diana,* "in spite of much incidental beauty, was habitually wanting in interest, except in so far as it renounced its pastoral nature."[7] It is indeed possible that by injecting aspects of sociohistorical truth in his novel Montemayor wanted "entramar con armonía la Poesía y la Historia—los dos polos temáticos y antitéticos de la poética neoaristotélica."[8] A recent sociological study by Joan Rockwell asserts that "the patterned connection between society and fiction is so discernible and so reliable that literature ought to be added to the regular tools of social investigation."[9] May I suggest that Montemayor's *Diana* should and indeed must be used precisely as such a tool for a greater understanding and appreciation of Spanish Renaissance culture?

The moral virtues embodied in the shepherds of *Diana* serve to contrast their "intrinsic nobility" with the villainy of other social groups. As honorable, faithful, and charitable, the shepherds are examples to be emulated by a public preoccupied with nobility and social status. To be considered, too, is the fact that the shepherds, like the workers of the land, were seen as "Old Christians," uncontaminated by Jewish or Moorish blood, and that because of this men and women sought shelter in the soul of rustic figures.[10] This may explain, in part at least, the idealization of the shepherds in *Diana* and the virtual absence of negative traits among them. After all, as Américo Castro notes, for the individual of the time to seek refuge in the soul of bucolic characters it was first necessary to make of their soul a worthy and habitable mansion.[11] Understandably, Rachel Bromberg in her perceptive consideration of the visionary aspects of *Diana* concludes that "it is less relevant for the reader to believe or disbelieve that what happens actually occurred in the dream world, or even that it might have occurred there, than for him to be impressed with the interest of the story itself and its hierarchy of worth governing behavior."[12]

1. Cited by Zeraffa, *Fictions,* 107.
2. Siles Artés, *Arte de la novela pastoril,* 162.
3. Émile Zola, *Le Roman Experimental* (1880), in *Les Oeuvres Complètes,* 46 (Paris, 1928): 46.
4. Fermín Estrella Gutierez, *Nociones de historia de la literatura española, hispanoamericana y argentina* (Buenos Aires, 1954), 67.
5. M. Romera-Navarro, *Historia de la literatura española* (New York, 1928), 206.
6. Marinelli, *Pastoral,* 73.
7. Walter W. Greg, *Pastoral Poetry and Pastoral Drama* (New York, 1906), 154.
8. Avalle-Arce, *La novela pastoril,* 95.
9. Joan Rockwell, *Fact and Fiction: The Use of Literature in the Systematic Study of Society* (London, 1974), 3–4.
10. *De la edad conflictiva* (Madrid, 1972), 221.
11. Ibid.
12. *Three Pastoral Novels,* 75.

With her draught Felicia cements the relationship between Sireno and Sylvano, which was already established at the beginning of Book II, where they are seen greeting each other with words of great friendship (68). At novel's end Sylvano is wedded to Selvagia, and their successful union appears to be the fulfillment of a longing the shepherdess once expressed to nature: "¡O, alta sierra, ameno y fresco valle / do descansó mi alma y estos ojos! / dezid: ¿verme [he] algún tiempo en tanta gloria?" (66).

The finality of *Diana*'s pilgrimage of love is marriage. As Felicia tells the shepherds and shepherdesses gathered at her palace, "el fin de vuestros amores será quando por matrimonio cada uno se ajunte con quien dessea" (228). In contrast to the amorous quests seen in many chivalric novels, "the adulterous and clandestine elements of courtly love are conspicuously absent" in Montemayor's work,[13] where, in addition to Sylvano and Selvagia, Felix marries Felismena and Arsileo takes Belisa as his wife. At all the marriages Felicia officiates as a symbol of Christian divinity, consonant with decisions of the first period of the Council of Trent in 1547, which stipulate that matters of marriage are to come solely under ecclesiastical jurisdiction.[14]

Marriage had already appeared as a viable solution to amorous frustration in the story told by Selvagia about Ysmenia, Montano, Alanio, and Sylvia. Now marriage becomes an event of the present, an influence on the conclusion of the novel and on its overall social and ideological intentions, intentions similar to those of morality plays, which "are characterized primarily, by the use of allegory to convey a moral lesson about religious or civic conduct."[15] The final marriages, then, are not "brought about by arbitrary magic, being merely an extraneous device with no particular significance apart from that of providing a happy ending."[16] The spiritual symbolism

13. Wardropper, "The *Diana* of Montemayor," 138. Cf. Justina Ruiz de Conde, *El amor y el matrimonio secreto en los libros de caballerías* (Madrid, 1948).

14. Jacqueline Savoye de Ferreras, "El mito del pastor," *Cuadernos Hispanoamericanos* 308 (1976): 39.

15. David M. Bevington, *From Mankind to Marlow* (Cambridge, Mass., 1962), 9.

16. Amadeu Solé-Leris, "The Theory of Love in the Two *Dianas*: A Contrast," *Bulletin of Hispanic Studies* 36 (1959): 79.

pervading the description of events at Felicia's palace converts what may seem superficially to be a mise-en-scène for conventional courtly love into a profoundly Christian setting. Milton, an avid reader of the pastoral, perceives this when, in his reflections on the genre, he remarks: "For he certainly whose mind could serve him to seek a Christian prayer out of a pagan legend, and assume it for his own, might gather up the rest God knows from where; one perhaps out of the French *Astrée,* another out of the Spanish *Diana.*"[17] After their "education" within the pastoral setting and their rebirths in the sacred Temple of Diana, the characters, with their newly acquired wisdom, are prepared to reemerge unto the common-sense world where they may love with "the purest and most noble kind of love,"[18] an illuminated end to a Christian pilgrimage and a vivid reminder of the novel's moral-didactic intention.

17. Milton, *Complete Prose Works* (New Haven, 1959), 3: 366-67.
18. Mary M. Lascelles, "Shakespeare's Pastoral Comedy," in *More Talking of Shakespeare,* ed. J. Garrett (New York, 1959), 75.

Index

Mary of Hungary, 38
Mary Tudor, 26
"Masking in Arden" (Davis), 103
Mendoza, Rodrigo de, 4
Menéndez Pelayo, Marcelino, 1
Menéndez Pidal, Ramón, 8, 11
Milton, John, 73, 109
Minerva (goddess), 59
Minerva, Temple of (in *Diana*), 23,
  41, 48, 86
Minturno, Antonio, 70–71
mirror as symbol, 64
"mito del pastor, El" (Savoye de
  Ferreras), 13
moderation, 62–63
Modoin de Autun, 4
Montano (in *Diana*), 17
Montemayor, Jorge de: *Cancionero*,
  4, 26, 85; *Carta de los trabajos
  de los reyes*, 4, 51, 61, 63, 102;
  Diálogo spiritual, 4, 55, 73, 81,
  84–85; "Egloga tercera a la
  señora doña Isabel Osorio," 26;
  *Exposición moral sobre el salmo
  LXXXVI del real profeta David*,
  61, 75, 84; *Glosa de diez coplas
  de Jorge Manrique*, 4; *Pasión de
  Christo*, 66; *Segundo cancionero
  espiritual*, 68, 88; *Los siete libros
  de la Diana*, passim.
"Montemayor's *Diana*: A Novel
  Pastoral" (Johnson), 37
Moreno Báez, Enrique, 53
Mucius Scaevola, 32
music, 18, 23, 39–40, 43, 87–92
myrtle tree, 15, 62

narcissism, 64–65
*Nature and Art in Renaissance Litera-
  ture* (Tayler), 2, 63
Neoplatonism, 42, 74, 82, 87, 89–90,
  92–93, 99, 101
New Christians, 3
*Nociones de historia de la literatura
  española* (Estrella Gutierez), 106
noon. *See* heat of the day
novela pastoril, La (Avalle-Arce), 99
nymphs (in *Diana*): as court ladies,
  23–24; as musicians, 23–24; as
  harmonizers, 71

Oaten Flute, The (Poggioli), 48, 65,
  74
"obra inédita, Uma" (Martins), 81
"O papel da palavra na *Diana* de
  Jorge de Montemor" (Cirurgião),
  20
Orations (Themistius), 26
Orator (Cicero), 85
Orfeo (Poliziano), 79
Orígenes de la novela (Menéndez
  Pelayo), 1
Orpheus, 33–34, 44–45, 79, 87–93
otiosus, 4
Ovid (Publius Ovidius Naso), 41

Paedogogus (St. Clement), 89
Pan (god), 12
Panofsky, Erwin, 64, 100–101
Panzacchi, Enrico, 10
Paradise Lost (Milton), 73
Paradiso (Dante), 100
Pasión de Christo (Montemayor), 66
Pastoral (Marinelli), 24
"Pastoral: A Literary Inquiry"
  (Greg), 10
Pastoral and Romance (Lincoln), 48
Pastoral Art of Robert Frost, The
  (Lynen), 24
Pastorale (Beolco), 40
*Pastorale, La: Essai d'analyse
  littéraire* (Gerhardt), 25
Pastorale Dramatique en France, La
  (Marsan), 34
Pastoral Novel, The (Squires), 24
Pastoral Poetry and Pastoral Drama
  (Greg), 5–6, 106
patriotism, 34
Pauluccio (singer), 9–10
Pèlèrinage Renart, 70
pensamiento de Cervantes, El
  (Castro), 99, 104, 107
"Peregrino de amor, El" (Vilanova),
  67
Pérez de Guzmán, Fernán, 33
Perry, T. Anthony, 99, 103
Petrarch (Francesco Petrarca), 5, 32,
  33, 92
Philip II (of Spain), 2, 26, 33, 38, 40,
  55
Philip III (of Spain), 26